SANITY ASSASSIN

Published in January 2010
in an edition of 300 numbered copies
to accompany the first UK exhibition of
Sanity Assassin, 2010, by Amanda Beech,
at Spike Island, Bristol, UK.

No .........

Special thanks to all of the contributors of this publication.
'The Thanatosis of Enlightenment', by Ray Brassier, reprinted with kind permission
of Palgrave Macmillan.

ISBN: 978-0-9553087-6-5

Printed by Divus.
Design & typesetting by coloursandstyles.

Published by Urbanomic,
The Old Lemonade Factory
Windsor Quarry
Falmouth TR11 3EX
United Kingdom

www.urbanomic.com

SANITY ASSASSIN

AMANDA BEECH

URBANOMIC
FALMOUTH

CONTENTS

INTRODUCTION

Sanity Assassin charts a new body of work initiated by artist, Amanda Beech. As part of her ongoing investigations into the forceful rhetoric played out within neo-liberal narratives of freedom in philosophy, politics, literature and popular culture, the artist has shifted her focus to the archetypal neo-liberal power base of Los Angeles. Researching on location, Beech has examined the city's historic and contemporary hegemonic narratives, the ideologies that have produced them and their current condition; an ethics of violence underscored as territorialisation, security and protection.

Sanity Assassin acts as a reader for a project that also exists in another form, as an eponymous three-channel video installation with a sculptural element; a spotlit mirrored plinth which displays a series of polished chainsaws situated in a custom-designed waiting area. This glamorous structure, with subliminal horror movie overtones, is an homage to the corporate lobby of a real Los Angeles showroom. Beyond is a three-screen video installation that embodies another violence: Hard-edged, uniform edits set to a pulsating noise score present a series of forced entanglements between architecture and nature, subjectivity and ethics, theory and practice, all pulled together in a claustrophobic journey through LA city space.

This book articulates a narrative through the art work in its research, construction and conclusion, with three informal parts bringing the images, texts and ideas through which the work was developed together with new points of discussion and reflection on the work's subject matter and contexts. The first part, *Dreamstuff*, takes the form of a discussion between Beech and artist and writer Jaspar Joseph-Lester. Joseph-Lester reflects on Beech's face-to-face interview with the late Julius Shulman a few months before he died. Aged ninety-eight, but still irrepressibly in command of his own legend as the architectural photographer of postwar LA mansions and housing tracts, Shulman, as Joseph-Lester observes, created both 'a system for generating images and his own myth making'. Exercising the total control of an auteur-director, he conjured up idealised representations to create the perfect foil for these luxury private spaces delineated by concrete, metal and glass. As a man with no time for theory, maintaining that there is only what 'you can see', Shulman's radical 'realism' was also fraught with contradictions.

Writer and lecturer Suhail Malik presents us with an essay, *Civil Society Must Be, Like, Totally Destroyed*, that evokes yet another version of California – not Shulman's mid-twentieth-century idyll, but a twenty-first-century failed state: bankrupt, in thrall to a low tax regime, unable to fund public education or healthcare, and with an ever burgeoning prison industry. Malik reads the psychosis of capitalism at work in California through two key Foucauldian terms: 'governmentality', in which social control is internalised, and 'biopolitics', in which political power is enacted on every aspect of human life. *Infinite Banalities*, a series of location shots made by Beech in LA during research for *Sanity Assassin*, shares the territories of Malik's essay. These bleak, epic spaces allude to the liberal convention that in order to make meaning in space one must designate authorship of it.

The second part of the book focuses on images, texts and narratives that featured in and fuelled the research for this project. It begins with philosopher Ray Brassier's essay *The Thanatosis of Enlightenment*, adapted from the groundbreaking *Nihil Unbound: Enlightenment and Extinction*, where Brassier explores the stark consequences of Adorno and Horkheimer's seminal text *Dialectic of Enlightenment*. Brassier offers a uniquely anti-humanist perspective on Adorno and Horkheimer's critique of scientific reason, advocating the destitution and destruction of the anthropomorphic subject. *Adaptation* features a series of photographs and montages that expands this focus on correspondence theories and their aesthetic, fictional and political manifestation; the images range from the decadence of relativist dogmatism, as seen in the postmodern architecture of the LA Cathedral of Our Lady of the Angels glowing subterranean crypt, to the horrific consequences of Dr Xavier's (Ray Milland) collision with the Real in *"X" The Man With The X Ray Eyes*.

Robin Mackay, philosopher and editor of *Collapse: Journal of Philosophical Research and Development*, begins the final part of the book with a short work of theory-fiction, *The Horror in the Library*. Mackay's text excavates the terrain of the video work and installation *Sanity Assassin* to generate another narrative that speaks to a concern central to the work: the fears that subtend dialectical reason, and the horror it awakens. Mackay's fiction, however, takes another route through this foray into the torments of reason. Echoing Beech's characteristic textual conflation of the rhetoric of reason and the brute force of pulp fiction, he collages H.P. Lovecraft's cosmic horror, with its isolated protagonists and malignant forces, together with Adorno's dark and haunted later writings, which reflect on the catastrophic events of the industrialised twentieth century. The narrative weaves these voices in and out of synthesis through dark corridors, delirious dreamscapes, and claustrophobic bourgeois interiors. Whilst never completely merging the two (Adorno's and Lovecraft's nightmares, after all, assigned radically different roles to the racial 'other'), Mackay mimics their respective hyperbolic theatrics with due black humour, leaving the reader to decide whether the delirium at the heart of the story is the hysterical symptom of a lonely exile or the index of a real, unspeakable horror lurking beneath human history. The constrained nature of this choice – the choice between private fiction or immanent fact – spells out the true horror of dialectical reason.

A discussion of the operations of reason, critique and power occupies the final part of the interview between Beech and Joseph-Lester, *Reason Without Reason*. The theme of self-constraint delivered in Mackay's fiction is expanded upon here in a questioning of how art participates in reconfiguring what is understood to be our 'commonality', the violence that this hope implies, and the force of its execution. Here the core foundations of a liberal-critical art practice are put on trial. This is most significant when we ask how (and if) art is capable of producing new agreements that transform and dissent from those that are considered to be established, institutional and, by their very nature, exclusive, when the standards of critique are not exempt from and often construct these conditions. These questions are considered in a discussion of the wider implications of Beech's project in the context of neo-liberal politics, normative claims for the operations of art, and the possibilities for a critique that can take these systems into account.

The book concludes with *Sanity Assassin*, a series of stills taken from the video work. Shulman's psyche enters directly into *Sanity Assassin*, as does the voice of Adorno through Beech's reworking of his *Dream Notes*, which were written almost daily during his time in exile in America. Shulman and Adorno act as the starting points for textual transmissions that deliver the inner psychologies of two central characters, whose divergent philosophies ultimately merge into one nihilistic polemic. Their radical individualism and uncompromising ideological positions lead to either dark suicidal horror or pure physical violence, the former expressed in the lurid colours of a distorted nature where funereal flowers succumb to the decompositional horror of their enculturalisation, the latter in the aesthetics of a disorientated mind that unleashes itself as the physical manifestation of the truth of nature.

Beech's interest in the conventions of reason, the form and affect of false and ideal realisms, and the structures of ontological formations, are evident throughout the work as well as in the various inquiries within this book. *Sanity Assassin* thus explores what the artist terms 'exclusion as power', acknowledging that the paradigm of security manifest in LA's architecture and its cinematic counterpoints is also alive and well in that other realm of the image, the art world.

Marie-Anne McQuay, Curator, Spike Island

DREAMSTUFF

Amanda Beech & Jaspar Joseph-Lester

Julius Shulman, *David House*, Lake Arrowhead, 1960

JJ-L: There is a photograph by Julius Shulman (*David House*, Lake Arrowhead, 1960) that is taken from inside a mid-century modernist Californian house near Los Angeles. The landscape outside is framed by a large set of doors and windows. In the photograph the building is used as a tool for mediating the landscape or, more specifically, as a framing device for rendering nature cinematic, constructed and idealized. Like many of Shulman's images, the hard modernist lines of the building speak of architectural space as a system for generating what we might call an image space. The landscape has the look of a painted backdrop and, like the interior, it appears as a stage waiting for something to happen. In this photograph there exists a whole series of images. It is as if the David House is the product of a catalogue of fragmented images, pasted together by Shulman to form an uneasy singularity.

When you were researching *Sanity Assassin* in Los Angeles, you went to visit Shulman in his house. I remember you saying that he asked you what you saw in the photograph that hung above his desk. Or, if I remember correctly, he demanded that you respond to his question: 'What do you see?' You mentioned that this question was repeated a number of times, as if there was some kind of secret within the image for you to decipher.

AB: My meeting with Shulman was driven by the question of the place of modernist idealism within his work; after all, he spent a lifetime producing images of the houses that re-interpreted this idealism for the US psyche. The informal interview took place in his studio, which is attached to his house in the Hollywood Hills, a few months before he died. I think we have to remember that Shulman was around ninety-eight years old and had worked his muscle in the world of interviews for the best part of the last century. I knew that Shulman was rehearsing the same points that I'd come across in other interviews, and these theatrics drove home the hubris and self-determination that were the overwhelming impression left by this meeting.

His question 'What do you see?', I think, comes from his deep scepticism of theorising in itself. This is Shulman's deliberate philistinism. The kind of answer he wanted was one that would 'say it like it is': the kind that stops thought in its tracks. This reliance on hard realities is connected directly with his critical interpretation of the romantic tendencies in architectural modernism, the architecture he documented throughout this career. He said that the socialist- and Euro'-inspired dreams of LA architects like Richard Neutra were just 'dream stuff' and that they never saw reality as it was.

I think it's best to describe the picture a little first. The picture uses an infrared film that turns the sky a stormy black. Shulman used this in a lot of his work. The left of the photograph, which is around eight feet long and five feet high, is taken up with the edifice of an LA modernist build, shot at an oblique angle. Through the glass we can see a couple of easy chairs and the scene looks down onto the sea, the beach and the town below to the right. His question 'What do you see?' is the kind of question that only he would know the answer to, despite his apparent intention only to describe available facts. This is the big secret and the great cover-up of Shulman's realism. What I mean by this is that Shulman's anti-idealism discloses another idealism. First of all because his call to 'say what you see' can never be satisfied by a correct response. In fact, this call to description is a means for Shulman to tell us the big answer that only *he knows* and which is part of his own theory of picture-making as well as how this architecture worked in terms of its politics. Of course, we could put it down to Shulman's interest in controlling the interview situation, but this also points to a wider issue of power. This idealism, then, is based in the secret of Shulman himself, in the kind of subjectivity that has a supposedly natural relationship to constructing image and to the spaces within which it works. Shulman talked about the naivety of photography students who took cameras to shoots and looked through the lens. For him, he said 'it's all in here' prodding at his own head. 'This is the camera'. For me, this naturalisation of thinking and making became central to understanding the type of realism encountered in Shulman's work.

Julius Shulman in his studio,
Hollywood Hills, California, USA

This is a picture of Shulman taken in his studio, sitting in the same seat where I interviewed him. In the background you can see the photograph.

By the way: The answer is 'the sea'. But the sea for Shulman is representative of the big ideal itself. This focus seems to override any socialist-inspired architectural plans that might have thought through the possibilities of building for communities, such as those of Charles and Ray Eames and Gregory Ain, because it describes a concept of singularity – an individual connection to nature that, whilst being universalised, is not communal. This emphasis on singularity leads to my second point: The sea is never just the sea, it is always a metaphor – and here, it becomes the lynchpin for *the* social ideal. The ideal for the life of 'the one' is to be close to that vast nature. Shulman connects this demand to the town in the image, Redondo Beach, which lies south of Venice Beach. He said that the dream failed because the ideal was to live with sea views, to be close to that experience of nature. This was impossible, since in the built-up overpopulated ad-hoc architecture and town planning of Redondo, all that neighbours can see is each other and *more architecture*. This is the fault of architectural planners. The idea of living in nature can only be maintained as a concept, because at home there is no real access to it. Community destroys it. The dream house on the hill could only exist because it was exclusive. Such exclusivity offers the only access to that dream in a material/visual sense. The relationship to nature in its particular and abstract form therefore becomes both the measure of the good life and the yardstick for an engagement with reality for the inhabitants of LA. This overarching investment in proximity is something that Shulman still invested in.

People have said that Shulman's works reflect the hopes for an entire age, but what are these hopes? And how does this architecture figure in them? There's also a lot of review-style writing about the importance of the human figure within his work, and that in photographs where there are no humans we still feel a human presence. But what I think is interesting about Shulman's work is its formalism, or its attempt to get rid of the opposition between architecture and nature or man and nature. This is a collision with the risk and chance that only nature can offer, but presented in a hard world. In his photography people are equivalent to flowers, to oranges, vases, or trees. They are *other objects* in a world of strange equivalences. People are colour or props, and in these values we can see a breaking down of identities into materialities that produce their own systems. You mention this in your observation about the 'pictures within pictures' that you see in his work. These fragments, tableaux, or mise-en-scene(s) can be taken as various systems of relations that work across the picture. The order that we encounter in the first instance is made up of objects, which, although part of the image, also engender a mystical or even cultic quality to the work. It is here that Shulman's realism sets up something that is more than nature: it invites an excess.

JJ-L: Could we then argue that the excess or surplus that exists in Shulman's photographs reflects his attempt to restage modernism? It's as if the world that Shulman records has been constructed within a giant movie theatre, ready to be documented under the most appropriate conditions. In this role Shulman can be seen as an über-architect presiding over those romantic apprentices earnestly reformulating their deluded offerings – Something like Howard Roark (played by Cary Grant) in King Vidor's cinematic interpretation of Ayn Rand's *The Fountainhead* (1949), when he says: 'my work is done my way, nothing else matters to me ... I live by the judgment of my own mind and for my own sake'.

In a similar way, we can perhaps also imagine Steve Wynn shouting that down from one of his mega-casinos in Las Vegas; but instead of the modernist belief in originality (that Roark and Shulman are determined to live by), Wynn directs architectural space as if it is a series of images for people to move through. These themed spaces each make some claim to be a transformative destination; they compete for our attention and pull us in different directions. Wynn understands the relationship between image, identity and belief and feeds our desire for differentiation – even if it is a visible construction.

Like the players that are cast into the themed reproduction of Venice, Egypt, Paris or Rome in Las Vegas, or like the community that is hired in for the sake of continuity in Peter Weir's *The Truman Show* (1998), Shulman is only interested in treating people, as you say, like props: they are always equivalent to the inanimate objects that surround them. When you were researching *Sanity Assassin* in Los Angeles, you visited a number of locations for the shoot, such as Mar Vista, Mulholland Drive and The Getty Institute, and I know that one of the main interests you have in Los Angeles is how it is represented not only by its architecture, and how this designates space and society, but also how images of Los Angeles participate in this construction of identity. Would it be fair for us now to speculate that Shulman's big secret is the central role of the photographer in the image: what we see in Shulman's photograph hanging above his cluttered desk is Shulman? Here again he takes command of nature – making it flat, turning the sea black, framing views, etc. – and situates it at the heart of the image. In this photograph, nature speaks of Shulman's idealism. In this way he is a lone subject determining the world as he sees it. The reality that Shulman argues for is a space purged of humanity; and this negation leaves the landscape free for him to occupy and possess. The images of LA that Shulman is so famous for recording not only manipulate and restage the landscape, they are the construction of a particular set of beliefs; they are a manifestation of the artist himself. However, this is no secret. It is more the case that this construction is floating in a sea of images that make some claim to document or represent Los Angeles or even to possess some truth about it. Is it then the moment when these representations, narratives or even identities come into conflict with one another; when they begin to disrupt a sense of singularity or cohesiveness. Is it this point of rupture that interests you?

AB: This return to an intact subjectivity and the theme of will is central to the discussion of Shulman's work, but in a wider sense it also allows us to think about the theme of the subject in theory and culture, where, as you say, although the theme of representing the subject is dismissed as Romantic, what is actually driven forward is a transcendental subjectivity which authors the 'world' we encounter in the work, and forms fragments into discrete ontologies. It gets more interesting when we approach spaces and theories that seek either to evacuate the need for a central figure or subject that would give us the satisfaction that we might 'mean' something in a universal sense, or to present us with a world that is not 'for us'. In that sense Shulman's work pushes beyond the dynamics of *The Truman Show*, because there is no designated reality inside the frame. The point of reality in the film is not only the architect of this reality (the crazed TV producer with a God-complex) but also Truman himself. Love and desire are also written as the forces that quash the false realities that govern Truman's world. Whereas with Shulman, the reference point for such a reality is not disclosed or focussed on in any such way. We feel the force of reason *through* the work rather than its being the work's subject matter. This dynamic, I think, extends to Steve Wynn as the author of much of Las Vegas's economic infrastructure and public aesthetic. What I think is so interesting about Wynn is that he worked hard to make the Vegas that we know, with pirate shows, dancing fountains and the 'world-as-theme-park'-style extravagance. This is the Vegas where you are immersed in the worlds made for you: worlds where everything is accessible, amenable, and available. This world, as you say, has systems of competing distractions that seem to fully understand the demand of neo-liberal subjectivities. What also fascinates me about Wynn is the phenomenon of the new Wynn casino empire. Unlike his other earlier casinos, like *Treasure Island, The Wynn*, which is just a little way further up the strip, is a place of more sedate seclusion and private luxury. The Ferrari dealership is now out back and the fountains are on the inside. It's almost as if Wynn's change in focus to the luxury market accepts the fact that participation and inclusion are not egalitarian conditions for experience. Egality is just another concept that leads the market to produce different forms of consumer experience. Reading Pine and Gilmore's book *The Experience Economy* (1999), as we know, has told us this already.

However, as soon as you're out there on the street, walking down the strip, there's that feeling of alienation and bleak disorientation, quite unlike the disorientating pleasure that you can get inside those distracting interior spaces. Vegas only works when you're participating directly in its economy; when you're out on the street you're a waste of time to Vegas, because this world, constructed with the processes of disorientation and even alienation in mind, has its boundaries. In this I perceive a disconnect between the construction of alienation and the form of alienation you get when you're just not playing.

Still from Amanda Beech, *We Never Close* (single channel video work, 8 mins, 2007).

I think your question, which asks about the effect of other people's worlds on us, and about how ontological claims have force upon us, is crucial here. The issue that comes up in your question is: How can we have a realist proposition of world without idealising our relation to it? What you identify is that in Shulman's critique of modernity's notion of the world being for us, we encounter instead the world that is authored by us, an encounter which impresses on us the power of will and mastery. So that this attempt to understand our relationship to nature as something that is simply 'there' ends up, for Shulman, with nature being something that is dissected, transformed, territorialized and organised. The subject's relation to the sea, then, is never one of equivalence.

It is formal and ideal. This may leave humanity outside his conception, outside the frame, in representational terms; but it is through this exclusion that his work embeds a form of egoism in the image, an egoism that speaks to the force of a particular kind of realism. This point of view is psychological, private and claustrophobic, a withdrawing from the world in hubris. This almost reactionary withdrawal, segmentation of space and privacy is perhaps strangely comparable to the work of Critical Theory, and this is where we can draw some parallels between the dialectic of reason and nature written through Theodor Adorno and Max Horkheimer's work.

CIVIL SOCIETY MUST BE, LIKE, TOTALLY DESTROYED

Suhail Malik

Freedom in the regime of liberalism is not a given, it is not a ready-made region which has to be respected. [...] Freedom is something that is constantly produced. Liberalism is not the acceptance of freedom; it proposes to manufacture it constantly.

[...] What then will be the principle of calculation for this cost of manufacturing freedom? The principle of calculation is what is called security. The problem of security is the protection of the collective interest against individual interests. Conversely, individual interests have to be protected against everything that could be seen as an encroachment of the collective interest. [...] Strategies of security, which are, in a way, both liberalism's other face and its very condition, must correspond to all these imperatives to concerning the need to ensure that the mechanisms of interests does not give rise to individual or collective dangers.[1]

In early to mid-July 2009, California looked like it was going to fail to reach a Budget agreement for the following fiscal year. The effects of such a failure would have been catastrophic with state workers not being paid, schools closing, public welfare and healthcare services withdrawn, construction and municipal services grinding to a halt, all of which would have added to the already severe damage inflicted upon the

---

1. Michel Foucault, *The Birth of Biopolitics: Lectures at the Collége de France, 1978-79,* trans. Graham Burchell (Basingstoke: Palgrave, 2008), 65.

Californian economy by the then ongoing credit crunch. California was not alone amongst the US states in reaching a difficult point in squaring its finances:[2] all but a handful were in deficit over the 2008-09 fiscal year, hit by a combination of drops in income across the board – taxes from earnings, sales, capital gains, and corporate and property revenues falling markedly as a result of increased unemployment or job precariousness, reduced profits or business bankruptcies resulting from the credit crunch, and the collapse of the housing market – coupled with a concomitant increase in welfare, healthcare and other provision costs precisely because state support was needed more when the private sector took the hit. Iris Lav, the Deputy Director of the Washington-based Center on Budget and Policy Priorities, remarked that in general state budgets in the US are 'moving from the damaged to the devastated'. But even in this general malaise of state-level functioning in the US, in which nine states face 'fiscal peril', California's problems are 'in a league of their own' with the lowest bond ratings of any of the American States indexing a rapidly declining confidence on its continued fiscal viability.

Although the drama of the Budget crisis of Summer 2009 brought California State's parlous situation to the headlines, its problems are enduring and unresolved. They are generated by the contradictory double demand highlighted in the citation from Michel Foucault above: that in liberalism the State 'produces freedoms' by limiting itself, yet such freedoms can only be sustained with guarantees of security against the dangers they themselves pose to the continued viability of the collective interest. Three points follow from this general formula of liberal governance:

- Including freedom from government as a task and production of government is a more expansive notion of governmentality than its direct identification with State power. With liberal governmentality, the constraint to political power is an internal constraint of government, and this 'internal constraint' is not only the freedom but also the security it offers.[3]

---

2. Details in this paragraph are from Jennifer Steinhauser, 'Facing Deficits, States Get Out Sharper Knives', *The New York Times*, November 16 2008 [www.nytimes.com/2008/11/17/us/17fiscal.html?_r=1&scp=13&sq="california budget"&st=cse]; Tom Petruno, 'Study: Nine states risking California-style "fiscal peril"', *LA Times Money*, November 11 2009 [latimesblogs.latimes.com/money_co/2009/11/pew-study-california-states-in-fiscal-peril-arizona-nevada.html]; Kathy Robertson, 'State's bond rating downgraded, again', *Sacramento Business Journal*, July 6 2009 [sacramento.bizjournals.com/sacramento/stories/2009/07/06/daily19.html].

3. Foucault, 2008, 65.

- it should not be underestimated that liberal governmentality takes place as a literally *spatial* production of freedom: the privacy that is the other name for such freedom is most likely spatially organized as the domestic, the fenced-off, the interior of the mind, its thoughts, and so on - in general, an interiority distinct and secreted from an exteriority that can always ravish it.

- Contrasted to Europe, where the 'internal constraint' moderates or is incorporated by a pre-existing power (the monarch, State power before liberalism, the police state, and so on), liberal governmentality is the starting point for America, the reason and cause of its formation, its legitimizing principle: 'the demand for liberalism founds the state rather than the state limiting itself through liberalism'.[4] If America is famously the land of freedom, this freedom is obtained through the governmentality that secures the freedom of what is outside of government – that there *is* an outside of government.

The problem with this expanded notion of governmentality is how to establish the integrity of the space in which government and, in particular, the juridical rights it both establishes and subjects itself to, is established and co-exists consistently with the space and freedoms beyond it. These two domains are definitionally distinct in kind but one must leave the other free and so must somehow produce it and not claim it. Foucault identifies this most general practice of governmentality to be civil society:

> How can a reason, a rational principle be found for limiting, other than by right or by the domination of economic science, a governmental practice which must take responsibility for the heterogeneity of the economic and the juridical? [...] Civil society is, I believe, a concept of government technology [...] that makes a self-limitation possible for governmental practice and an art of government [...]; it makes possible a self-limitation which infringes neither economic laws nor the principles of right.[5]

---

4. Foucault 2008, 217.

5. Foucault 2008, 296.

Civil society is the general space of governmentality in which both freedom and security are managed *together*, as two heterogeneous moments of one production or what Foucault calls 'the same ensemble of technology of liberal governmentality' as a system of checks and balances between government, rights and economy without interference from government.

This settlement is coherent enough, and continues to be consensually affirmed since the beginning of the American experience of constitutional self-government through the common vibrancy of its civil society, market, and juridical checks and balances on governmental power. But what is the content of this external dimension of freedom? Why is it necessary at all? Foucault's genealogy accounts for it as the space of market and economic transactions, the production of a reason that, in this logic, is best served the more government exempts itself from its operation and it is exempted from government. And here the case of California is instructive, for what it shows all too clearly is that the validation of economic freedoms has in fact given rise to the corrosion of the *general* principle of liberal government as Foucault determines it. What is now complex, as signaled by the specific conditions and decisions of how and why California stays in a condition of financial peril, is that the 'principle of calculation' of security for any such government is now itself dis-integrated under two incompatible requirements, one stemming from its formation in checking individual and collective securities against each other, and another from private capital accumulation that takes a privileged site as the realm of freedom that government must sustain (not least, for its own survival). This complexification, it will be seen, undoes the liberal settlement of civil society from within the very terms on which it is premised, pitching it against itself in a turn characteristic of neo-liberalism.

Within California State's fiscal policy it is Proposition 13 that most famously encapsulates the turn of liberal governmentality against itself. Brought on to California's Statute books in 1978 as a result of one of the State's direct democracy initiatives, wherein propositions can be put to common plebiscite through the legislature or upon presentation of a petition with a minimum of about 8 percent of active voters, Proposition 13 (i) requires California's government, alone amongst American states, to have a 'super-majority' of two-thirds of its legislature to approve any increases to tax rates, and also (ii) limits property taxes to 1 percent of the property's assessed value, to increase by a maximum of 2 percent a year thereafter. Here it is private wealth through earnings and property – private capital accumulation – that is the realm of a freedom at once liberated from government and for which government also provides security against 'collective dangers' through the super-majority requirement. The medium-to-long-term costs of such freedom to public finances have been dire: since revaluations of assessed value are only permitted when property changes ownership, aside from distorting property taxes by duration of ownership rather than property value, revenue from property taxes is pretty minimal and effectively negative when annual inflation exceeds 2 percent, as has been the case for most of the period between its implementation and early-mid 2009. And with just more than one third of California's legislature in the hands of Republicans, the super-majority requirement established by Proposition 13 makes the initiative system a route taken frequently by the legislature as well as private citizens to raise taxes. It also makes the State's tax system hard to coherently rationalize since, aside from making it impossible for the legislature to raise tax revenue by simple majority, several of the stipulations made by various propositions are contradictory.

Faced then with shortfalls in long-standing regular expenditures and constrained in how to effect Budget cuts, two options remain: cuts to core services and increasing revenues through consumption taxes and bond issues. These were the options taken by the State legislature and endorsed by Governor Arnold Schwarzenegger in arriving at the $100 billion Budget in Summer 2009. Cuts amounting to $15.6 billion included:[6]

- $6.5 billion from pre-high school education over the 2008-10.

- $1.3 billion from the state supported health service for the poor.

- $1.2 billion from the state prison system, leading to the release of 27 000 inmates.

- $510 million from the state's welfare-to-work programme.

- $50 million from a programme providing health insurance to children from low-income families.

- $124 million from the health insurance programmes for the children of the poorest.

- $2 billion from non-dedicated funds to the State's university system.

- not paying state workers three day per month, saving salary costs of $425 million over two years.

---

6. Matthew Garrahan, 'California spending cuts spark fury', *Financial Times*, July 21 2009 [www.ft.com/cms/s/0/bde67fd8-75b2-11de-a9d8-00144feabdc0.html]; Legislative Analyst's Office, July 2009 Budget package, July 29 2009 [www.lao.ca.gov/laoapp/PubDetails.aspx?id=2112]; Jesse McKinley, 'Denied Tax Revenues, Local Officials in California Are Fuming', New York Times, July 21 2009 [www.nytimes.com/2009/07/22/us/22local.html?_r=1&scp=7&sq=%22california%20budget%22&st=cse]; Christopher Caldwell, 'California's Fiscal Charade', *Financial Times*, July 24 2009 [cachef.ft.com/cms/s/0/27fc634c-7879-11de-bb06-00144feabdc0.html].

Many of the cuts were made from the General Fund, monies not ear-marked to particular expenditures. Schwarzenegger added a further $500 million of cuts in a line-by-line veto of the Budget put to him by the legislative houses including:[7]

- $80 million that was to pay workers helping abused children.
- $50 million from services for children under three with learning disabilities.
- $16 million from supporting domestic-violence victims.
- $6.3 million from services for the elderly.
- $6.2 million from parks forcing maintenance drawbacks.

These almost comically villainous cuts to public services for the most vulnerable were accompanied by increases in revenue sought from:[8]

- Borrowing $2 billion from local county and city taxes (which fund road and other infrastructural repairs).
- $12.5 billion tax increases, including a quarter percent on personal income tax, 1 cent on sales tax and increasing vehicle taxes to 1.15 percent – propositions that failed to be approved in the initiative ballots required by Proposition 13 but nonetheless raises income for two years.
- Selling State property.
- Approving oil-drilling off the coast for the first time since 1969 to generate resource taxes.
- Trading the State debt on credit markets through bond issues.

7. Michael Rothfeld and Shane Goldmacher, 'Schwarzenegger cuts $500 million more as he signs budget', *LA Times Local,* July 29 2009 [www.latimes.com/news/local/la-me-california-budget29-2009jul29,0,7361988.story]; California Budget Project, *Uncharted Waters: Navigating the Social and Economic Context of California's Budget*, May 2009 [www.cbp.org/publications/state_budget_land.html].

8. California Budget Project, op.cit.; McKinley, op.cit.

Bond issues are regularly used by governments at all levels to raise short-term cash by selling their debt with the promise of buy-backs with varied interest levels according to the duration of the bond. California's bond issues to the $2.8 trillion municipal bond market are worth detailing[9] because they highlight a chronic governmental expenditure, an enduring dynamic of systematic financial loss, from government to structured private capital markets. This slow drain of public finances is well recognized by critics of the link between government and private wealth accumulation. What is less obvious is that such accumulation is related to but distinct from the property tax limitations established by Proposition 13 as an initiative stemming from the space of freedoms guaranteed by governmental self-constraint and, as such, an effect of liberal governmentality. While variable, this effect is nonetheless persistent: for instance, since its Budget crisis California's bond issues have had declining success:

- September 2009: $9.2 billion of orders were placed for $8.8 billion of bonds, much of the demand coming from private retail buyers. The relatively low interest rates of 1.25 - 1.5 percent for bonds with maturities up to nine months, costing the State a total $15.5 million in net interest, compare well for the purchaser with the near zero interest rates set by the Federal Reserve, and also for the issuer against interest rates of 3.75 – 4.25 percent for similar bond issues a year prior.

- October 2009: the issue of $4.5 billion of bonds with maturities of 20 years was cut back to a total of $4.14 billion and interest rate yields boosted from 4.63 percent to 5 percent to increase their attractiveness to unwilling purchasers.

- November 2009: yields on bonds issues maturing over four or so years are increased from 2.48 percent to 4 percent annualized and tax-free.

---

9. Nicole Bullock, 'California debt sale draws retail interest', *Financial Times*, September 24 2009 [www.ft.com/cms/s/0/b49a3b5a-a8ab-11de-9242-00144feabdc0.html], 'California debt sale disappoints', *Financial Times*, October 8 2009 [www.ft.com/cms/s/0/6f6b3d52-b3a2-11de-ae8d-00144feab49a.html and 'California cuts size of bond deal', *Financial Times*, October 9 2009 [www.ft.com/cms/s/0/426d4ac6-b45f-11de-bec8-00144feab49a.html]; 'No Free Lunch', California Budget Project, November 12 2009 [californiabudgetbites.org/]; Tom Petruno, 'California debt binge shakes up muni bond market', *LA Times Business*, November 10 2009 [latimesblogs.latimes.com/money_co/2009/11/california-muni-bond-sale-tax-free-market-yields.html].

This decline in the attractiveness of the bond issues reflects changes in the bond markets themselves, which had rallied somewhat by October 2009, but it also reflects that despite states being usually rated at 'AAA' status, since they are perceived to not default on bonds (they can in principle always raise taxes to cover any losses), California is rated at 'A' – and even down to 'BBB' by one agency at the time of the Budget lockdown – that is, just above junk bond status and close to if not at the bottom of the ratings of American states. Pride aside, the ratings matter because lower ratings, which index the supposed security of the bond being repaid, mean that, to attract buyers, higher yield interest rates need to be in place to outweigh the greater risk indexed by the lower rating or when bond issues saturate the demands of the municipal bonds markets – or both, as happened over early Autumn 2009 with over $21 billion of bonds issued by California over the preceding two months. And higher yields constrain long- and medium-term budget decisions since they oblige greater outgoings from the State towards bond markets against other obligations.

The requirement to service the refinancialisation of government debt has been presented in some detail for California because it makes manifest in particularly stark form the problem of the incoherence between two distinct kinds of security – and so two different 'principles of calculation' of freedoms – that underpin the freedoms of liberal governmentality. For the state *must* ensure its own security as a viable creditor by meeting its yield payments. Without such credit-worthiness, any agency loses its capacity to raise money on bond markets, making it impossible to raise short-term capital to pay for immediate needs and cover other shortfalls. States are then obliged to meet the capital and interest repayments on their bond issues as a matter of priority. Furthermore, although bonds are able to raise money for immediate use quickly and relatively cheaply, servicing the debt and paying interest becomes an increasingly significant obligation on government treasuries. In California, such obligations are paid from the same General Fund from which shortfalls in budgets dedicated to schools, healthcare, welfare, parks and recreations are met. Assuming moderate growth in the economy, debt servicing on bonds approved through the initiative plebiscite system is projected by California's treasury to increase from 6.7 percent to 10.2 percent of the total revenue income in the five years from 2009, staying at that share of total revenues to about 2028. While such figures indicate on their own the costs of the State's obligations to the bond markets, these obligations of course do not exist independently of the State's other commitments. More specifically, increased levels of debt servicing not only place greater strain on the State's budget if the economy weakens (since the overall income to the State then shrinks, leading to a further reliance on bond issues to cover shortfalls and so increasing debt servicing costs…) but, more tellingly, the proportion dedicated to repaying debt increases as the strain on the State's social functions and expenditure itself grows because of worsening general economic conditions.

What California then makes explicit, because of the dramatic circumstances in which its shortfalls have come to public attention, coupled to the increasing share of debt servicing it consequently takes on as a result, is a common enough requirement for governments now: namely, that the security liberal governments provide for the 'free spaces' they manufacture is *practically* oriented towards the freedom of private markets for capital accumulation. *This* security is crucial to governments themselves because it enables them to continue functioning by refinancing their debts through bond issues to those private markets. And it is a security that comes at the literal cost of the security of the population as a whole, which is for Foucault the biopolitical subject of govern-mentality characteristic of the modern period, in which power shapes the production of life (health, insurances, education, and so on). For California, faced with a further shortfall of $1.1 billion by November 2009 on top of the $7.4 billion planned into the 2009-10 budget because of reduced tax income – a shortfall itself due to falling property prices and real wages, declining corporate tax, the shrinking back of personal consumption, record levels of unemployment because of recession, and legal reversals to Governor Schwarzenegger's last minute cuts to services to the elderly, the selling-off of the State's work insurance scheme, and county level protection of their property tax base from State level appropriation ($2 billion of property tax repayments paid for by the 4 percent yield November bond issue mentioned above)[10] – the biopolitical security of liberal governmentality is classically organized along the lines of the following exemplary provisions:[11]

- An increase of just over a third of a million Californians receiving food stamps in the year to end-2008, a 17 percent increase over a year to a total of just over 2.5 million people.

- A two-year increase of over 110 000 children to the State's children's health services scheme.

---

10. Kevin Yamamura, 'Governor blames budget woes on judges "going absolutely crazy"', *The Sacramento Bee,* October 22 2009 [www.sacbee.com/politics/story/2272576.html?mi_rss=State%2520Politics]; Shane Goldmacher, 'New billion-dollar hole in California's budget', *Los Angeles Times Local*, October 9 2009 [latimesblogs.latimes.com/lanow/2009/10/new-billion-dollar-hole-in-californias-budget.html].

11. California Budget Project, *Uncharted Waters*; 'Regional and State Employment and Unemployment Summary', Bureau of Labor Statistics, US Dept of Labor, October 21 2009 [www.bls.gov/news.release/laus.nr0.htm]; 'Employment Situation Summary', Bureau of Labor Statistics, US Dept of Labor, November 6 2009 [www.bls.gov/news.release/empsit.nr0.htm]; California Budget Project, *In the Midst of the Great Recession: The State of Working California 2009,* September 2009.

-   An increase of 82 percent claiming unemployment insurance in the two years to June 2009, to a total of just over a third of a million people.

But this last-mentioned insurance gives a concrete example of the literal impoverishment of California State funds for once core biopolitical provisions: faced with an increase in unemployment rates to a record 12 percent (compared to a national average of 10 percent), and job losses returning the total number of jobs in California back to levels comparable to those prior to the 2000's boom even though the State's population had grown by over three million in the intervening period, the increase in claimants for unemployment insurance – payments to cover basic needs through the depredations of joblessness – cost the State over $1 billion in June 2009, nearly three times the amount from two years earlier. Since the State kept little in its Unemployment Insurance reserves over the period of the boom of the preceding decade, that fund became insolvent in January 2009. To continue paying the Insurance it is legally obliged to, the State borrowed close to $3 billion in seven months from the federal government (money itself available through taxation and bond issues). If these trends continue and no extra income is raised to pay for this Insurance, the debt due to this one factor alone is projected to reach close to $18 billion by end-2010.[12]

The rapid increase in claimants of Unemployment Insurance, and the State's fiscal incapacity to meet the social demands of its worst-off at a time of greatest need, attest to something of the transformation of the liberal settlement identified by Foucault in the late 1970's, just as neo-liberalism was consolidated in the richer countries through the Reagan and Thatcher conservative revolutions. It encapsulates in stark terms the constant threat of public insolvency that must be met on a contingent and occasional basis by government obtaining short-term funds from other government agencies and also private markets. The profits gained by private markets from such borrowing is a direct transfer of public money to private finance, a transfer of wealth into the hands of those with enough investment capital to maintain the basic functioning of the State – as an in-principle public entity by ownership but also as a public recourse. Abstracting a little further, public funds form a profit base for the private finance sector (operating in this case though the municipal bond market), a profit that *increases* the more the government falls short of meeting even its basic operating costs, at the price of internal insolvency for its most necessary social insurance funds. Liberal governmentality corrodes biopolitical social security.

This logic, which captures the practical neo-liberal engagement of private markets and government, can be put the other way around: public service obligations can only be met *because* of the ability of private capital, structured through exchange markets,

---

12. California Budget Project, *In the Midst of the Great Recession*, 8.

to provide the funds to meet them. This version justifies and legitimates neo-liberal market conditions as a social good, not just for the individual who benefits from it directly through capital accumulation but also for government, which recognizes it as a condition for the provision of some social security for its people *and*, as played out on a much larger scale with the internationally co-ordinated government bail-out of the credit system over 2008-09, for the private capital markets. Pushed a step further, the logic proposes that government is only a mediator between the efficient accumulation of capital through market exchange and the unfortunate but necessary fall-out of those who don't do well from such enterprise. The money to support such enterprise – channeled to the worst-off or most needy through government – becomes cheaper to lend and borrow the more of it there is around, hence the necessity to liberate income and profit from taxation and other non-market based charges as much as possible, since these siphon capital away from its true home in private markets. With another turn of the screw, this logic also explains why over the period[13] the tax burden proportional to income has become much greater for the poorer (who service the entrepreneurs) than for the richer (who use their capital and also generally don't need state services anyway) – 11 percent for the lowest-earning fifth of Californians compared with 8 to 9 percent for the top fifth – and average pre-tax income gains have been much greater for the richest – nearly 11 percent for the poorest fifth of Californians over the decade to 2006, dropping to 8.5 percent for the middle fifth, rising dramatically to 45 percent for the top fifth with the top 1 percent increasing their gross income by close to 110 percent: ten times the increase of the poorest fifth. In sum, and typically of neo-liberal regimes, the poorest who need social security and public services the most not only contribute to the tax base proportionally more of their income, they are also hit hardest by cutbacks to those services during downturns, reductions effected because of an overall relative reduction in taxation for corporations and the richest segments of the population. This logic is consolidated the less tax is paid by the wealthiest and business, and the more government must borrow to cover its shortfalls because of the shrinking of that tax base.

The liberation of earnings from tax – of private income from public services – is perhaps the key controlling logic of California state's fiscal (dis)organization, not just as it is enacted through the various ideologically-charged initiative plebiscites and power plays within its legislature, but also within the quotidian-pragmatic machinations of how the State raises the money to continue funding its services. Tax cuts in California since 1993 amounted to a reduction of $12 billion in tax income for 2008-09 alone and over $10 billion for every year since 2005-06, contributing to the long-term trends and systemic constraints that force cuts in budget allocations supposed to guarantee

---

13. California Budget Project, *Uncharted Waters*.

some minimal security for the poorest to the point of insolvency. One-off solutions to this or that payment crisis distort future budget commitments adding to the systematic growth of the core imbalances as does the increasing volume of debt servicing. One example is the reduction of corporate tax revenues by close to $9 billion for most of the decade up to 2020 then reducing this revenue stream by a further $2.5 billion per year; a demand made by the Republican party as part of a deal to allow passage of 20 other unrelated bills requiring super-majority approval.[14]

Beyond the specifics of California's numbers, the dynamics presented here have been well established in general terms since the Reagan and Thatcher revolutions in the early 1980s, coming to fruition through the Washington Consensus of the 1990s and reaching a devastating plateau with the credit crunch of the mid-late 2000s.[15] In terms of Foucault's analysis of liberal governmentality, what is effected in California's continued financial 'peril' and the specifics of its generation and allocation of revenues is more caustically yet a destruction of civil society by government subject to the sovereignty of capital accumulation which is, per force, outside of it. With Foucault, neo-liberalism does not belong to the settlement of classical liberal governmentality, but attacks it on the basis of its own conditions. Neo-liberalism does not remain within the terms of settlement between the subject of rights and the economic subject but models the 'overall exercise of political power […] on the principles of a free economy'.[16] That is, neo-liberalism takes the free market to be the truth of governmentality in general, its sole criterion. With American neo-liberalism the market assumes dominance, takes a sovereignty which is no longer political but economic:

> In classical liberalism the government was called to respect the form of the market and *laisser–faire*. Here, *laissez-faire* is turned into a *do-not-laisser-faire* government, in the name of a law of the market which will enable each of its activities to be measured and assessed. *Laissez-faire* is thus turned around, and the market is no longer a principle of government's self-limitation; it is a principle turned against it.[17]

---

14. California Budget Project, *Uncharted Waters*; George Skelton, 'GOP's "leverage" is tantamount to extortion', Capitol Journal, *LA Times Local*, September 17 2009 [www.latimes.com/news/local/la-me-cap17-2009sep17,0,1524376.column].

15. Marxist elaborations of this history can be found in David Harvey, *A Brief History of NeoLiberalism* (Oxford: Oxford University Press, 2007) and, more thoughtfully, in Peter Gowan, *The Global Gamble* (London: Verso, 1999).

16. Foucault 2008, 131.

17. Foucault 2008, 247.

With neo-liberalism the freedom of the economic subject becomes the very condition by which it usurps and condemns that which constrains itself to produce such freedoms. Neoliberalism destroys the 'ensemble of technology of liberal governmentality' and puts it under the command of free market.

This somewhat Oedipal situation is not the abolition of government or the subject of rights as such but their subordination to the truths of free market requirements positivised as scientific fact, principles presented as the neutral fact of yields, spreads and returns. And this is a destruction of civil society insofar as that term signals the settlement between the subjects of political sovereignty, rights and the economy through the self-limitation of government. This destruction is specific and consistent; it is shaped by the organization of the free market for capital accumulation which is sovereign over its truth. That sovereignty is by necessity not a political one if politics is identified, as it is in this schema, with the subject of government, since it is constituted precisely on the basis of the freedom that it takes to be given independently of government rather than produced by its self-restraint, a freedom that then understands itself to be prior to its political formation and strives to maintain itself in that priority.

Adorno Construction Inc., Campbell, California

www.adornoconstruction.com

The ideological and pragmatic aspects of this weakening of the state as a primarily social-collective undertaking – in its ideal, of the public as it represents and supports itself to and for itself – are consolidated through the systemic constraints and long-term trends facing California's State budget, the consequences of which are repetitiously evaded by the short-term, dramatic – and therefore news-format friendly – last-ditch pulling back from insolvency. What this dynamic enacts is the domination of the freedom propounded in the free space of capital markets and the security they require for continued fiscal returns (up to and including higher yields for riskier investments such as California), a domination that practically corrodes the social security that is the principle of calculation for the freedoms of the classical liberal settlement of civil society. The danger realized by neo-liberalism to the classical formation of liberalism is not that of a collective interest overwhelmed or endangered by individual interests, which is a problem of classical liberalism, but that of a general collective interest corroded by and subjugated to the particular collective interest of the advance of capital accumulation, whose naturalized subject is the individual assumed to be free in their capital accumulation (a conjunction characterizing neo-conservatism).

This destruction of civil society cannot be undone or recuperated by an appeal to a stronger or better-defended civil society, since that is the very condition for the formation of the neo-liberal attack on the security that civil society offers, to which neo-liberalism is indifferent other than as object of critique. Rather, it is the very condition upon which neo-liberalism is premised and which enables it to have its sovereign command over political sovereignty, the very separation of the subject and domains of government, rights, and economy, that must be destroyed in order to maintain security for populations who do not benefit from the sovereignty of capital accumulation but who, since capital is necessarily accumulated differentially,[18] are subjugated to the depredations it necessitates. And this also requires a destruction of civil society: not the partial destruction inflicted by neo-liberalism in order to enact its own sovereign demands (without government as domain of political sovereignty, neo-liberalism's own domination is extinguished) but its *total* destruction. That is, in the unwinding of the settlement between freedom and security that has been modern liberal governance, the prospect of a future dominated by capital accumulation or not is contingent on the vanquishing of one destruction of civil society by another. And this is a question of whether and how the spaces of private freedom are to be constituted.

---

18. Jonathon Nitzan and Shimshom Bichler, *Capital as Power: A Study of Order and Creorder*, (London.NY: Routledge, 2009).

THE THANATOSIS OF ENLIGHTENMENT

Ray Brassier

Myth and Enlightenment

Myth is already enlightenment; and enlightenment's destruction of superstition-
merely reinstates myth: such is the speculative thesis proposed by Adorno and
Horkheimer's *Dialectic of Enlightenment*.[1] This dialectic of myth and enlightenment
is structured around an entwinement of mimicry, mimesis, and sacrifice which not
only underlies the book's 'excursus' on Odysseus and its chapter on anti-Semitism,
but arguably also furnishes it with its fundamental conceptual core. Though each
of these concepts are undoubtedly complex, and mobilized for distinct purposes
in different parts of Adorno's oeuvre in particular, their deployment in *Dialectic of
Enlightenment* seems to harbour the key to this speculative thesis. If, as Andreas
Huyssen suggests, the concept of mimesis functions in five 'distinct but nevertheless
overlapping' registers in Adorno's work,[2] three of these are fully operative in
Dialectic of Enlightenment: the anthropological register; the biological-somatic
register; and the psychoanalytic register. The argument of *Dialectic of Enlightenment*
weaves these three registers together while distinguishing between mimicry, which
ostensibly has a negative connotation in the book, and mimesis, whose speculatively

---

1. Theodor Adorno and Max Horkheimer, *Dialectic of Enlightenment,* tr. Edmund Jephcott
(Stanford: Stanford University Press, 2002) [DoE].

2. Andreas Huyssen distinguishes these five registers as follows: '[F]irst, in relation to the
critique of the commodity form and its powers of reification and deception, a thoroughly
negative form of mimesis [*Mimesis ans Verhärtete*]; secondly, in relation to the anthropological
grounding of human nature which, as Adorno insists in *Minima Moralia*, is 'indissolubly
linked to imitation'; third, in a biological somatic sense geared toward survival, as Adorno had
encountered it in Roger Caillois's work […]; fourth, in the Freudian sense of identification and
projection indebted to *Totem and Taboo*; and, lastly, in an aesthetic sense that resonates strongly
with Benjamin's language theory, as it relates to the role of word and image in the evolution of
signifying systems.' Andreas Huyssen, 'Of Mice and Mimesis', *New German Critique, No. 81,
Dialectic of Enlightenment* (Autumn 2000), 66-7.

positive sense may be glossed as 'similitude without conceptual subsumption'. At the same time, the concept of sacrifice assumes its decisive import for the book's speculative thesis as the paradigm of non-conceptual exchange. The entwinement of similitude without identity and exchange without subsumption provides the pulse of the dialectic of myth and enlightenment.

Thus Adorno and Horkheimer's thesis might be paraphrased as follows: The sacrificial logic of myth is repeated in reason's own compulsive attempt to overcome myth by sacrificing it: enlightenment reiterates mythic sacrifice by striving to sacrifice it. But in doing so it unwittingly mimics the fatal compulsion which it intended to overcome. Only by 'working through' the sacrificial trauma that drives rationality – a working through which is characterized in terms of reason's reflexive commemoration of its own natural history – can reason renounce its pathological compulsion to sacrifice and thereby become reconciled to the part played by nature within it. True demythologization – the dialectical resolution of the opposition between myth and enlightenment – would then coincide with the relinquishment of the sacrificial drive to demythologize; or in Adorno and Horkheimer's own words: 'Demythologization always takes the form of the irresistible revelation of the futility and superfluity of sacrifices' (DoE 42). Reason becomes reconciled to nature by sublimating its compulsion to sacrifice myth. In this regard, *Dialectic of Enlightenment* attempts to fuse Hegel and Freud in what can only be described as a 'dialectical psychoanalysis' of Western rationality.

But everything hinges on the manner in which mimicry, mimesis, and sacrifice are dialectically entwined. More precisely, *Dialectic of Enlightenment*'s speculative coherence depends on the feasibility of maintaining a rigid demarcation between mimicry and mimesis, sacrificial repression and enlightened sublimation. If organic mimicry reduces to adaptation, then it falls under the aegis of identity, and anthropological mimesis can be confidently contrasted to it as a harbinger of non-identity: correspondence without a concept. But this neat distinction is far from assured. In the fragment entitled 'Toward a Theory of the Criminal', Adorno and Horkheimer explicitly identify mimicry with the death-drive: '[Criminals] represent a tendency deeply inherent in living things, the overcoming of which is the mark of all development: the tendency to lose oneself in one's surroundings instead of actively engaging with them, the inclination to let oneself go, to lapse back into nature. Freud called this the death-drive, Caillois *le mimétisme*' (DoE 189).[3] But how is this explicit identification of biological mimicry with the death-drive related to the following cryptic formulation from the excursus

_____

3. Adorno had reviewed Caillois's 1934 text 'La Mante religieuse' (originally published in *Minotaure 5* [1934]: 23-6) in the *Zeitschrift für Sozialforschung* 7 (1938): 410-11. Also relevant in this regard is Caillois' 'Mimétisme et psychasthénie légendaire', originally published in *Minotaure 7* (1935): 4-10, which we will discuss below. Both texts are included in Caillois's *L'Homme et le sacré* (Paris: Gallimard, Folio/Éssais, 1988) (first published in 1938). English versions can be found in *On the Edge of Surrealism: A Roger Caillois Reader*, C. Frank and C. Naish (eds) (Durham: Duke University Press, 2003).

on Odysseus, which seems to identify the latter with mimesis rather than mimicry?: 'Only deliberate adaptation to it brings nature under the power of the physically weaker. The reason that represses mimesis is not merely its opposite. It is itself mimesis: of death' (DoE 44). This could be paraphrased as follows: in sacrificing the mimetic impulse (blind conformity to nature, the compulsion to repeat) in order to ensure human survival, instrumental reason fatally repeats its own submission to nature. It has to mimic death in order to stave it off. This would seem to encapsulate the nub of the dialectical critique of instrumental rationality; a critique which identifies the latter as the root cause of Occidental civilization's precipitation toward self-destruction. But there is another sense in which it also harbours the germ of this critique's non-dialectical reversal: mimesis may have distinguished itself from mimicry, but mimicry does not distinguish itself from mimesis. For the genitive 'of' in reason's mimesis of death may plausibly be taken to be objective as well as subjective. As we shall see, the fatal reversibility of mimicry and mimesis, though denounced by dialectical reflection, is latent in the enigma of mimicry's non-adaptive *thanatosis* – what Caillois called its 'assimilation to space', which transforms reflection itself into a purposeless instrument and signals the technological destruction of critique. Thanatosis signals the fatal equivalence whereby the logic of mimesis reverses into mimicry, and critical negativity into the annihilating positivity of reason, which the reflexive dialectic of myth and enlightenment had sought to stave off.

The Sacrifice of Sacrifice

According to Adorno and Horkheimer, enlightenment reason is driven by an inexorable drive to conceptual subsumption which subordinates particularity, heterogeneity, and multiplicity to universality, homogeneity, and unity, thereby rendering everything equivalent to everything else, but precisely in such a way that nothing can ever be identical to itself. Thus conceptual identification stipulates a form of differential commensurability which, in Adorno and Horkheimer's own words, 'amputates the incommensurable' (DoE 9). 'Instrumental rationality' names an anthropological pathology expressing a materially indeterminate yet ubiquitous 'power', whose sole determination consists in its differentiation into dominating and dominated, rather than the result of any historically determinate configuration between conditions and relations of production. In the speculative anthropology proposed by Adorno and Horkheimer, instrumental reason is the extension of tool-use and hence a function of adaptational constraints. The emergence of instrumental rationality is inseparable from the primordial confrontation between dominating and dominated power, which primitive humanity experienced in its powerlessness before all-powerful nature. Sacrifice is the attempt to effect a commensuration between these incommensurables; between the omnipotence of nature and the impotence of primitive humanity. Yet from the outset sacrificial magic presupposed the logic of mimesis: 'At the magical stage dream and image were not regarded as mere signs of things but were linked to them by resemblance or name. The relationship was not one of intention but of kinship. Magic like science is concerned with ends but it pursues them through mimesis, not through an increasing distance from the object' (DoE 7). Mimesis establishes the equivalence between dissimilars which provides the precondition for sacrifice. It provides a non-conceptual commensuration of particularity with generality, thereby allowing one to serve as a substitute for the other:

> Magic implies specific representation. What is done to the spear, the hair, the name of the enemy, is also to befall his person; the sacrificial animal is slain in place of the God. The substitution which takes place in sacrifice marks a step toward discursive logic. Even though the hind which was offered up for the daughter, the lamb for the firstborn, necessarily still had qualities of its own, it already represented the genus. It manifested the arbitrariness of the specimen. But the sanctity of the *hic et nunc*, the uniqueness of the chosen victim which coincides with its representative status, distinguishes it radically, makes it non-exchangeable even in the exchange. (DoE 7)

Sacrifice's magical power consists in establishing a correspondence between things for which no *ratio*, no proportion of conceptual equivalence, yet exists. This is its quite literal *irrationality*. More importantly, mimetic sacrifice establishes the fundamental distinction whose rationality Adorno and Horkheimer believe enlightenment is in the process of eliding: the distinction between animate and inanimate: '*mana*, the moving spirit, is not a projection but the preponderance of nature in the weak psyches of primitive peoples. The split between animate and inanimate, the assigning of demons and deities to certain specific places arises from this pre-animism. Even the division of subject and object is prefigured in it' (DoE 11).

Moreover, if, as Adorno and Horkheimer argue, myth already exhibits the lineaments of explanatory classification which will be subsequently deployed in scientific rationality, then this distinction between animate and inanimate marks a fundamental cognitive accomplishment which science threatens to elide by converting all of nature into an undifferentiated material whose intelligibility requires a supplement of conceptual information. Scientific conceptualization mortifies the body: 'The transformation into dead matter, indicated by the affinity of *corpus* to corpse, was a part of the perennial process which turned nature into stuff, material' (DoE 194). Thus, Adorno and Horkheimer insist, 'the disenchantment of the world means the extirpation of animism' (DoE 2); enlightenment 'equates the living with the non-living just as myth had equated the non-living with the living' (DoE 11). Yet animism harboured a form of non-conceptual rationality precisely insofar as its practice of sacrifice established a principle of reciprocity between inanimate power and animate powerlessness. The rationality of sacrifice consists in this power to commensurate incommensurables: power and impotence, life and death.

The speculative fusion of Hegel and Freud undertaken by Adorno and Horkheimer would seem to imply three successive strata of mimetic sacrifice and three distinct registers of exchange between life and death. The first stratum, according to Freud's own excursus into speculative biology in *Beyond the Pleasure Principle*, would mark the emergence of the organism through the sacrifice which secures the relative independence of its interior milieu against the inorganic exterior. Part of the organism has to die so that it may survive the onslaught of the inorganic: the organism sacrifices its outer layer to the inorganic as a 'shield against stimuli'.[4] The second stratum would mark the emergence of mythic exchange as the stage at which humans learnt to sacrifice the animate in order to placate animating powers. According to Adorno and Horkheimer, this is the sacrifice that establishes a reciprocity between dominated and dominating, victim and gods, and hence represents a gain in human autonomy: 'If exchange represents the secularization of sacrifice, the sacrifice itself, like the magic schema of rational exchange, appears as a human contrivance intended to control the gods, who are overthrown precisely by the system created to honour them' (DoE 40). The third stratum would be that of the emergence of the self and the definitive separation between culture and nature. The permanence of the ego is secured against the flux of fleeting impressions through the teleological subordination of present satisfaction to future purpose: thus, '[t]he ego [...] owes its existence to the sacrifice of the present moment to the future. [But] its substance is as illusory as the immortality of the slaughtered victim' (DoE 41). But where sacrifice had previously served as a means for mastering external nature, it now becomes introjected as the suppression of the power of internal nature.

However, this sacrificial subordination of means to end in fact reverses itself into a subordination of ends to means, for in learning to repress the drives and desires whose satisfaction define it, the human organism effectively negates the ends for which it supposedly lives. For Adorno and Horkheimer, this marks the beginning of that dangerous substitution of means for ends, and of the reversibility between function and purpose, which they see as defining the reign of instrumental rationality and which attains its pathological apogee in what they describe as the 'overt madness', 'the antireason', of technological capitalism. Yet the roots of this madness were already present at the origin of subjectivity:

> The human being's mastery of itself, on which the self is founded, practically always involves the annihilation of the subject in whose service that mastery is maintained, because the substance which is mastered, suppressed, and disintegrated by self-preservation is nothing other than the living entity, of which the achievements of self-preservation can only be defined as functions – in other words, self-preservation destroys

---

4. Cf. Sigmund Freud, 'Beyond the Pleasure Principle' in *The Penguin Freud Library. Vol. 11: On Metapsychology* (Harmondsworth, Middlesex: Penguin, 1991) 270-338.

the very thing which is supposed to be preserved [...] The history of civilization is the history of the introversion of sacrifice – in other words, the history of renunciation. (DoE 43)

Thus enlightenment becomes the sacrifice of sacrifice; its internalization. The separation between nature and culture, discipline and spontaneity, is secured by becoming internal to the subject. But in order to secure it the subject must imitate the implacability of inanimate nature; it disenchants animate nature by miming the intractability of inanimate force: 'The subjective mind which disintegrates the spiritualization of nature masters spiritless nature only by imitating its rigidity, disintegrating itself as animistic' (DoE 44). For Adorno and Horkheimer, this furnishes the key to the fatal complicity between enchantment and disenchantment, myth and enlightenment. Enlightenment's pathological reiteration of the logic of mythic thought is exemplified in its exclusive regard for the immanence of the actual and its obsessive focus on the ineluctable necessity of the present:

> In the terseness of the mythical image as in the clarity of the scientific formula, the eternity of the actual is confirmed and mere existence is pronounced as the meaning it obstructs [...] The subsumption of the actual, whether under mythical prehistory or under mathematical formalism, the symbolic relating of the present to the mythical event in the rite or abstract category in science, makes the new appear as something predetermined, which therefore is really the old. It is not existence that is without hope but the knowledge which appropriates and perpetuates existence as a schema in the pictorial or mathematical symbol. (DoE 20-21)

Consequently, for Adorno and Horkheimer, the abyss that separates science's conceptual knowledge of the actual from 'existence' would be the abyss between the identical and the non-identical; an abyss of un-actual negativity whose inherently temporal structure only philosophical reflection is capable of recuperating. Reason can overcome its self-alienation from natural existence, suspend the oppressive immanence of absolute actuality and redeem the possibility of hope, only through the commemorative reflection of its own historicity. Given its crucial role in Adorno and Horkheimer's account, this denouement of the dialectic of enlightenment warrants quoting at length:

> Precisely by virtue of its irresistible logic, thought, in whose compulsive mechanism nature is reflected and perpetuated, also reflects itself as a nature oblivious to itself, as a mechanism of compulsion [...] In mind's self-recognition as nature divided from itself, nature, as in pre-history, is calling to itself, but no longer directly by its supposed name, which

in the guise of *mana* means omnipotence, but as something blind and mutilated. In the mastery of nature, without which mind does not exist, enslavement of nature persists. By modestly confessing itself to be power and thus being taken back into nature, mind rids itself of the very claim to mastery which had enslaved it to nature […] For not only does the concept as science distance human beings from nature, but, as the self-reflection of thought […] it enables the distance which perpetuates injustice to be measured. Through this remembrance of nature within the subject, a remembrance which contains the unrecognized truth of all culture, enlightenment is opposed in principle to power, [it has] escaped the spell of nature by confessing itself to be nature's own dread of itself. (DoE 32)

The reasoning here is impeccably Hegelian: mature reason achieves its independence from nature reflexively by remembering its own dependence upon it. But according to Adorno and Horkheimer, reflexivity is precisely that which science remains incapable of. If, as they maintain, 'all perception is projection' (DoE 154) – the mediation of sensible impressions by conceptual judgement – then an adequate cognitive reflection of things as they are necessitates bridging the abyss between sense data and actual objects, inner and outer. Thus '[t]o reflect the thing as it is, the subject must give back to it more than it receives from it' (DoE 155). But this is precisely what conceptual subsumption, whether positivistic or idealistic, is incapable of doing: 'Because the subject is unable to return to the object what it has received from it, it is not enriched but impoverished. It loses reflection in both directions: as it no longer reflects the object, it no longer reflects on itself and thereby loses the ability to differentiate' (DoE 156). Cognition becomes pathological when its projection excludes reflection. The privileging of reflection as the hallmark of rational sanity entails the pathologization of science's 'unreflecting naivety' as an instance of 'pathic projection' which merely differs in degree, rather than kind, from anti-Semitism: 'Objectifying thought, like its pathological counterpart, has the arbitrariness of a subjective purpose extraneous to the matter itself and, in forgetting the matter, does to it in thought the violence which will later will be done to it in practice' (DoE 159).[5]

---

5. The implication, more pathetic than provocative, is unavoidable: Einstein and Himmler are separated merely by degrees, not kind.

Commemorating Reflection

The upshot of Adorno and Horkheimer's critique is clear: reason's reflexive mediation is contrasted to its irreflexive immediacy as health is to sickness: 'The subject which naively postulates absolutes, no matter how universally active it may be, is sick, passively succumbing to the dazzlement of false immediacy' (DoE 160). Adorno and Horkheimer counterpose the healthy mediation of reflexive negativity to the sick mediation of total subsumption, just as they contrast reflexive consciousness' 'living' incorporation of qualitative particularity to the latter's annihilating consumption through mathematical formalization. In the final analysis, 'only mediation can overcome the isolation which ails the whole of nature' (DoE 156). And this mediation must take the form of remembrance: 'What threatens the prevailing praxis and its inescapable alternatives is not nature, with which that praxis coincides, but the remembrance of nature' (DoE 212). Such remembrance would aim at inaugurating a 'second nature': a nature mediated by human history and reinvested with the full apparel of human socio-cultural significance. Second nature would be nature reflexively incorporated and internally memorized – or, in the words of Jay Bernstein, 'the nature whose appearing to us is conditioned by our belonging to it'.[6] Bernstein's formula perfectly encapsulates the fundamental tenet of what Quentin Meillassoux has called 'correlationism', i.e., the claim that there is a necessary reciprocity between the human and the non-human, or mind and nature.[7] Correlationism hankers after second nature precisely insofar as the achievement of the latter would render material reality into a depository of sense fully commensurate with man's psychic needs. Moreover, if we accept Bernstein's suggestion that for Adorno 'the living/non-living distinction is the fundamental one',[8] then we begin to appreciate the extent to which the ultimate horizon of Adorno and Horkheimer's critique of scientific reason is the rehabilitation of a fully anthropomorphic 'living' nature – in other words, the resurrection of Aristotelianism: nature as repository of anthropomorphically accessible meaning, of essential purposefulness, with the indwelling, auratic *telos* of every entity providing an intelligible index of its moral worth. Underlying this philosophical infatuation with the lure of second nature is a yearning to obliterate the Modern (post-Cartesian) dissociation of knowledge from value; a nostalgic longing to reconcile the 'is' and the 'ought'; and thereby to 'heal' – since nature 'suffers' in its isolation from human contact – the Modern rift between understanding what an entity is and knowing how to behave toward it. This philosophical yearning for second nature betrays nothing less than a longing to revoke spirit's estrangement from matter, to reforge the broken

---

6. Jay Bernstein, *Adorno: Disenchantment and Ethics* (Cambridge: Cambridge University Press, 2001), 191.

7. Quentin Meillassoux, *After Finitude: An Essay on the Necessity of Contingency*, London and New York, Continuum 2008.

8. Bernstein 2001, 194.

'chain of being', and ultimately to repudiate the labour of disenchantment initiated by Galileo in the physical realm, continued by Darwin in the biological sphere, and currently being extended by cognitive science to the domain of mind.

The implicitly religious tenor of this reflexive commemoration of lost experience becomes explicit in its insistence on the redemptive value of memory. 'Reconciliation', Adorno and Horkheimer claim, 'is Judaism's highest concept and expectation its whole meaning' (DoE 165). Judaic monotheism is to be admired for managing to 'preserve [nature's] reconciling memory, without relapsing through symptoms into mythology', thereby prefiguring 'happiness without power, reward without work, a homeland without frontiers, religion without myth' (DoE 165). Judaism prefigures second nature precisely insofar as it provides a prototype of demythologised religion. But if the Judaic *Bilderverbot* (the prohibition of images) is the seal of rationally disenchanted religion, its reflexive rehabilitation as the prohibition of any positive conception of the absolute marks the apex of mystification; a mystification sanctified in the critical absolutization of the difference between the knowable and the unknowable, the finite and the infinite, immanence and transcendence – those very distinctions which science is deemed guilty of having disregarded. The critical interdiction of absolute immanence aims at the attainment of a second nature which would secure the reflexive redemption of the future on the basis of the present's commemoration of the past. The qualitative substance of experience supposedly obliterated by abstract conceptual form is retroactively projected as the irreducible material of socio-historical mediation.

But this substance of experience is itself a philosophical myth. For although the dialectic of myth and enlightenment may be formally plausible, it derives its substantive critical force from a conflation between dialectical form – exemplified in the analysis of the logic of sacrifice – and a positive content which is nothing but the retroactively posited residue of conceptual subsumption: the pre-conceptual experience of 'meaning' harboured in the perceptual apprehension of qualitative particularity. In this regard, Adorno and Horkheimer's thesis is vitiated by a constant slippage between two entirely distinct claims: viz., the claim that scientific reason has occluded a meaningful experience *of* nature, on the one hand; and the claim that it has obscured the experience of meaning *as* nature, on the other. To defend the first would involve a commitment to the primacy of some sort of pre-conceptual phenomenological understanding of nature – precisely the sort of stance precluded by Adorno and Horkheimer's Hegelian emphasis on the ineluctable socio-historical mediation of experience. To defend the second would be to relapse into the kind of reductive naturalism exemplified by contemporary evolutionary psychology, whose positivistic precursors Adorno and Horkheimer abhorred. Yet in spite of – or perhaps even because of – this emphasis on historical mediation, the meaningful particularity of forgotten experience, whether 'of' or 'as' nature, is evoked as the content which science has lost by abstracting from its alleged concretion. But this meaningful content is supposed to be at once qualitatively and positively substantive – experience in the full-blooded phenomenological sense – and the negation of subsumptive abstraction. What is this dimension of meaningfulness of which we have supposedly been deprived if it is neither positively given as a transhistorical invariant, nor some originary phenomenological datum, and if its determinate specificity is merely the shadow retroactively cast by its subsequent negation? Reflection provides the sole criterion of authentication for the memory that we used to have more than we have now, and this memory is all that can substantiate the claim that we have been deprived of something. But *whose* memory is it? In light of the critical prohibition of absolute knowledge, and hence of the inaccessibility of absolute knowledge's self-commemoration, how are we to gauge the reliability of Adorno and Horkheimer's speculative remembrance of human history? Dialectical commemoration should never be taken on trust. The 'experience' whose attenuation Adorno and Horkheimer lament seems to have no other substance than the one which reflection retrospectively imparts to it.

In fact, the invocation of remembrance reveals how Adorno and Horkheimer's critique of enlightenment is carried out from the perspective of the commemorative consciousness which feels its own existence threatened by the scientific occlusion of 'meaningful particularity'. The critique proceeds from the viewpoint of reflection, which is to say, commemoration. It is nostalgic for an experience whose substance mirrors its own longing. It is fuelled by the yearning for the mythic form of history as experience rather than for any specific or substantive historical experience. Thus it criticises the sacrificial myth of disenchantment by rehabilitating a fantasy of rational enchantment which betrays its own pining for the reflexive redemption of experience. Accordingly, and by its own lights, it is incapable of operating as an immanent critique of actual experience, since reflection is precisely what the actuality of instrumental rationality already *lacks*. But this lack is imputed to it on the basis of an appeal to a reflexively recuperated and transcendent past. Thus critique is conservation; moreover, it is structurally conservative since its commemorative reflection wishes to postpone temporal rupture in the name of continuity. The expectation of reconciliation retroactively forecloses the future prospect of temporal caesura. Reconciliation and expectation are the theological guarantors of redeemed nature. But science *has* no concept of 'nature', and this is precisely what dissuades it from stipulating any border between the natural and the unnatural: nature is neither more nor less than the various discourses of physics, chemistry, biology, geology, ethology, cosmology ... The list remains necessarily open-ended. Where the sciences of nature are concerned, the irreconcilable is their highest concept and the irremediable their only meaning. Paradoxically, it is in the concept of mimetic reversibility that this irremediability finds expression.

The Dispossession of Space

For Adorno and Horkheimer, the primary sense of biological mimicry would be that of an expression of the compulsion to adapt: organisms must either habituate themselves to their environment or perish. But mimicry in the biological sense spans a variety of different registers – from genetic replication, to behavioural compliance, to morphological imitation – none of which prove straightforwardly reducible to the logic of adaptation. It is this fundamentally non-adaptive character of mimicry which Roger Caillois draws attention to in his 1935 article 'Mimicry and Legendary Psychasthenia.'[9] In mimicking their own food, leaf insects such as the *Phyllium* frequently end up devouring each other. Their mimicry involves an uncanny teleplasty – a physical photography – which short-circuits any use-value the mimetic realism might have had by replicating even the physical symptoms of corruption and decay. Mirroring the necrosis of its own food, the *Phyllium* identifies itself as a dying semblance of its own living sustenance. The exorbitant accuracy of this insect teleplasty initiates an autophagy which becomes part of the organic coding of the physical photograph itself. Thus the symbiosis between the information of one organism – *Phyllium* – and another – leaf – undergoes an involution which simultaneously engenders the collapse of their identity and the erasure of their difference in the paradoxical convergence of organic verisimilitude and living death.[10] Mimicking the death of that from which it draws nourishment, the *Phyllium* becomes the living index of its food's decay for its own vital appetite.

Far from being an instance of adaptation, thanatropic mimicry marks the compulsion whereby the organism is driven to disintegrate into the inorganic. At the root of this thanatropism, Caillois suggests, is an attraction by space: organic individuation loses ground, 'blurring in its retreat the frontier between the organism and the milieu'[11] and becoming precipitated into a continuously expanding de-individuated space. Caillois proposes that this psychasthenic 'assimilation to space' is the common denominator underlying phenomena as apparently remote from one another as insect mimicry and schizophrenic depersonalization. Citing the work of Eugene Minkowski,[12] Caillois notes that the schizophrenic responds to the question 'Where are you?' with the claim:

---

9. Caillois 1988, 86-122.

10. I owe this formulation to Nigel Cooke's remarkable essay 'The Language of Insects' in *Sandwich 1: Autumn 2004* (London: SecMoCo Publishing).

11. Caillois 1988, 121.

12. 'Le problème du temps en psychopathologie' in *Recherches Philosophiques*, 1932-33, 239; *Le Temps vécue. Études phénoménologiques et psychopathologiques* (Paris: L'évolution Psychiatrique, 1933); *La Schizophrénie*, (Paris: Payot, Rivages, 1997) (originally published 1927); *Lived Time*, tr. N. Metzel (Evanston: Northwestern University Press, 1970).

'I know where I am but I cannot feel myself in the place where I find myself'.[13] Thus, schizophrenics are dispossessed of their psychic individuality by space:

> To these dispossessed souls space seems to be a devouring force. Space pursues them, encircles them, digests them in a gigantic *phagocytosis*.[14] It ends by replacing them. Then the body separates itself from thought, the individual breaks the boundary of his skin and occupies the other side of his senses. He tries to look at himself from any point whatever in space. He feels himself becoming space, *black space where things cannot be put*. He is similar, not similar to something, but just similar. And he invents spaces of which he is 'the convulsive possession'. All these expressions shed light on a single process: depersonalization by assimilation to space, i.e., what mimicry achieves morphologically in certain animal species.[15]

Ultimately, the pathology of instrumental rationality diagnosed by Adorno and Horkheimer would seem to be rooted in this psychasthenic dispossession by space, through which reason abjures the dimension of temporal transcendence which provided it with its capacity for reflexive commemoration. Reason becomes schizophrenic, and hence self-estranged, precisely insofar as it is evacuated of its temporal substance and rendered immanent to space. The psychosis of instrumental reason allows subjective reflexivity to be swallowed up in the brute opacity of the object. Yet thanatropic mimicry is the symptom of a non-conceptual negativity which is already at work among objects independently of their relation to subjectivity; a non-dialectical negativity which is not only independent of mind but realizes the indistinction of identity and non-identity outside the concept. In this regard, the thanatosis of enlightenment marks that point at which the transcendental subject of cognition is expropriated and 'objective knowledge' switches from expressing the subject's knowledge of the object to the object's knowledge of itself *and* of the subject that thinks it knows it. This intimate connection between thanatropic mimicry and objective cognition is one which Caillois had already identified:

> Accordingly, it is not only psychasthenia which resembles mimicry, but the imperative of cognition as such, of which psychasthenia in any case represents a perversion. As we know, cognition tends toward the suppression of every distinction, toward the reduction of every opposition, such that its goal seems to consist in presenting sensibility

---

13. Caillois 1988, 111.

14. *Phagocytosis* is a process describing the engulfment and destruction of extracellularly-derived materials by phagocytic cells, such as macrophages and neutrophils.

15. Roger Caillois, 'Mimétisme et psychasthénie légendaire', in Caillois 1988.

with the ideal solution to its conflict with the external world and hence to satisfy sensibility's tendency toward the abandonment of consciousness and life. In doing so, cognition immediately presents sensibility with a *calming image*, and one which is full of promise: the scientific representation of the world, in which the picture of molecules, atoms, electrons, etc., dissociates the vital unity of being.[16]

Yet Caillois' analysis continues to confine the thanatropism of cognition – and hence the dissociation of the 'vital unity of being' – to a subjective representation; as though the cleavage between representational image and represented world could remain immune to the dissociative virulence of this non-dialectical negativity. In fact, in anatomizing consciousness and life, the thanatosis of enlightenment not only dismembers the vital unity of being; more fundamentally, it objectifies the subject in such a way as to sunder the putative reciprocity between mind and world. It dispossesses the subject of thought.

The Mimesis of Death

This thanatropic dispossession at the hands of what Hegel referred to as the 'concept-less exteriority' of space explains the horror which mimicry inspires not only in civilization, but also in the dialectical reflection which purports to be the latter's witness. It is not surprising, then, that reflection charts the progress of civilization in terms of successive sublimations of the mimetic impulse – first through magic, in which mimetic logic provided the condition for sacrificial exchange; then with organized work, which marked its definitive prohibition: 'Social and individual education reinforces the objectifying behaviour required by work and prevents people from submerging themselves once more in the ebb and flow of surrounding nature' (Adorno and Horkheimer DoE 148). Civilization proscribes mimetic behaviour as a dangerous regression. This prohibition is at once social and conceptual: social, in that mimetic behaviour signals a weakening or loosening of egoic self-mastery and a regression to animal compulsion (which Adorno and Horkheimer see exemplified by the criminal); conceptual, in that mimetic semblance is an instance of similitude without a concept.

It is this latter sense that bears a particularly significant philosophical import for Adorno and Horkheimer. When something mimes something else, it becomes like it, but without resembling it according to any criterion of conceptual equivalence. Thus mimesis is an index of non-identity: it marks a register of indifference or indistinction operating independently of any conceptual criterion for registering identity or difference. Consequently, mimetic phenomena threaten both social order and conceptual order, exchange and subsumption. Yet the identitarian fear of mimesis

---

16. Caillois 1988, 119.

is mirrored by the terror which mimesis itself provokes. For Adorno and Horkheimer, both mimesis and subsumption are intimately connected to fear: a nexus of terror links civilization's fear of regression, the individual's fear of social disapprobation, the fear provoked by conceptual indistinction, and the prey's fear of its predator. Whether sameness is established conceptually, through the synthetic subsumption of particularity, or organically, via the imitation of the inorganic, it remains bound to terror. More precisely, the terror of mimetic regression engenders a compulsion to subsume, to conform, and to repress, which is itself the mimesis of primitive organic terror:

> Society perpetuates the threat from nature as the permanent, organized compulsion which, reproducing itself in individuals as systematic self-preservation, rebounds against nature as society's control over it [...] The mathematical formula is consciously manipulated regression, just as the magic ritual was; it is the most sublimated form of mimicry. In technology, the adaptation to lifelessness in the service of self-preservation is no longer accomplished, as in magic, by bodily imitation of external nature, but by automating mental processes, turning them into blind sequences. With its triumph human expressions become both controllable and compulsive. All that remains of the adaptation to nature is the hardening against it. The camouflage used to protect and strike terror today is the blind mastery of nature, which is identical to farsighted instrumentality. (DoE 149)

Thus mimetic phenomena are double-edged: mimicry is at once a defence mechanism and a weapon. It is exemplified by the prey's miming of the inorganic in order to evade the predator, but also by the predator's miming of its prey. But its ambiguity goes deeper, for it is the defence mechanism itself which converts into a weapon: the repression which served to preserve the organic individual against the threat of inorganic dissolution becomes its fundamental weapon against nature, whether organic or inorganic. Mimetic sacrifice effectuates a reversibility between the threatening power which is to be warded off, and the threatened entity which seeks to defend itself through sacrifice. It installs a reversible equivalence between dominating and dominated force, power and powerlessness, the organic and the inorganic. Ultimately, this reversibility renders the anthropomorphic vocabulary of fear and intimidation inappropriate: the organism's putatively defensive simulation of the inorganic – the horned lizard which simulates a rock – flips over into the inorganic's supposedly aggressive simulation of the organic – as in the case of viruses, which hijack their hosts' cellular machinery in order to replicate themselves. In disregarding this fundamental reversibility between mimic and mimicked, Adorno and Horkheimer ignore the return of mimicry within mimesis, and the possibility that anthropological mimesis itself may be a mask of mimicry. Though they recapitulate mimesis' anthropological and psychosocial aspects, they omit the first and arguably most fundamental stratum of mimetic sacrifice: the biological level, in which Freud grounded the compulsion to repeat in his account of the organism's emergence from the inorganic. Freud's biological construal of the death-drive remains an ineliminable prerequisite of Adorno and Horkheimer's account, for it explains the originary compulsion to repeat which is reiterated at the anthropological and psychosocial levels. Civilization's embrace of lifelessness in the service of self-preservation, its compulsive mimicry of organic compulsion in the repression of compulsion, reiterates the originary repression of the inorganic. Thus, if '[t]he reason that represses mimesis is not merely its opposite [but] is itself mimesis: of death' (DoE 44), this is because science's repression of mimesis not only mimes death, inorganic compulsion – it is death, the inorganic, that mimes reason. Mimesis is *of* death and *by* death. Life was only ever mimed by death; the animate a mask of the inanimate. The technological automation of intelligence which marks the consummation of self-destructive reason for Adorno and Horkheimer is nothing but the return of the repressed, not merely in thinking, but *as* thinking itself. Enlightenment consummates mimetic reversibility by converting thinking into algorithmic compulsion: the inorganic miming of organic reason. Thus the artificialization of intelligence, the conversion of organic ends into technical means and vice versa, heralds the veritable realization of second nature – no longer in the conciliatory aspect of a reflexive commemoration of reason's own natural history, but rather in the irremediable form wherein purposeless intelligence supplants all reasonable ends. Organic teleology is not abolished through reflection, but through synthetic intelligence's short-circuiting of instrumental rationality; a short-circuiting which overturns the sequential ordination of time and the future's subordination to the present by reinscribing time into space.

The horror which such a prospect provokes in dialectical thinking is intimately tied to the latter's desire to expunge space from history. Space is dialectically deficient because it remains mere concept-less self-exteriority. Thus, for Adorno and Horkheimer, the sequential ordination of space via narrative is the necessary precondition for the irreversibility of historical time: 'Laboriously and irrevocably, in the image of the journey, historical time has detached itself from space, the irrevocable schema of all mythical time.' (DoE 39) But the topological reinscription of history appals reflection because it threatens to dissolve memory back into the concept-less exteriority of space. Moreover, if synthetic intelligence consummates thanatropic mimicry, then enlightenment's topological reinscription of history does not so much reinstate mythical temporality as the dynamic of a horror story: human reason is revealed to have been an insect's waking dream.[17] The negative consummation of enlightenment signals the end of the dream of reason as codified in Hegelianism – for which the

---

17. In this regard, the veritable analogue for the dialectic of enlightenment is not Homer's *Odyssey* but rather David Cronenberg's *The Fly* (1986), whose protagonist declares: 'I was an insect who dreamed he was a man – and loved it – but now the dream is over and the insect is awake.'

reconciliation of mind and matter provided the *telos* of universal history – and the awakening of an intelligence which is in the process of sloughing off its human mask. Yet one way of underlining the profound philosophical import of Darwin's achievement would be to characterize it precisely in terms of this re-inscription of history into space. Natural history harbours temporal strata whose magnitude dwarfs that of the nature 'whose appearing to us is conditioned by our belonging to it' – for it proceeds regardless of whether anyone belongs to it or not. Even if it remains irreducible to it, cultural history is mediated by natural history, which includes both time and space, biology and geology. Disavowing the irreflexive immanence of natural history, Adorno and Horkheimer's speculative naturalism ends up reverting to natural theology. It is the failure to acknowledge the ways in which the socio-historical mediation of nature is itself mediated by natural history – which means not only evolutionary biology but also geology and cosmology – which allows philosophical discourses on 'nature' to become annexes of philosophical anthropology.

Saturday Night

Miramar Estates—Where Beverly Boulevard Meets the Sea

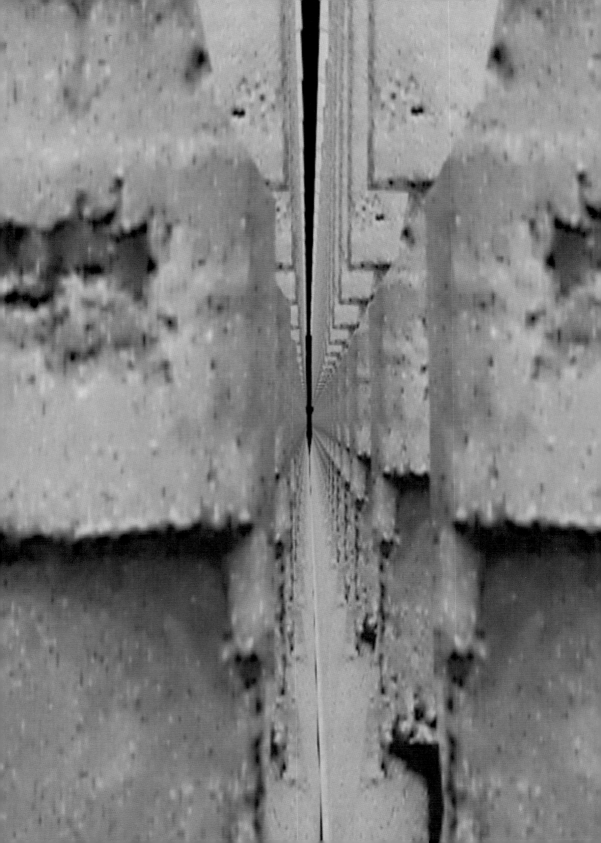

THE HORROR IN THE LIBRARY

Robin Mackay

Whether exaggerated suspicions are paranoiac or true to reality, a faint private echo of the turmoil of history, can only be decided retrospectively. Horror is beyond the reach of psychology.
Theodor Adorno, *Minima Moralia*

That is not dead which can eternal lie
And with strange aeons, even death may die.
 H.P. Lovecraft, *The Call of Cthulhu*

The most merciful thing in the world, I think, is the inability of the human mind to correlate all its contents. He who worries away at the impenetrable connections of alienated elements lays himself open to intimations which no individual mind can bear – knowledge too far beyond all the ideas of man to be believed except in the silent damnable small hours of the morning when one cannot sleep, those tormented hours drawn out without prospect of end or dawn, in the vain effort to forget time's empty passing.

In the ticking of the cheap mantel-clock, whose sound has come to seem like a thunder of artillery, I hear the mockery of light-years for the span of my existence. The hours that are past as seconds before the inner sense has registered them, and sweep it away in their cataract, proclaim that like all memory, our inner experience is doomed to oblivion in cosmic night.

It is only with vast hesitancy and repugnance that I am forced into speech – forced, because men of science have refused to follow my advice without knowing why. Having once attempted to bring my studies in tune with official scientific principles, I was soon to discover that those with whom this path mistakenly associated me would stop at nothing to insidiously attack and despoil the last retreats of resistance to their timorous and conformist probings. The type of culture I brought with me appeared to them to be unjustified arrogance. My reason rebelled at the flimsy logic with which they tried to gild their domineering competence with a sacredness stripped from the idols they had discarded. In turn, my nebulous and abstruse scribblings were derided for their 'factual errors' and 'colored opinions', slandered as irresponsible and barbaric. And yet, if there is an unbarbaric side of philosophy, it is its tacit awareness of the element of irresponsibility, of blitheness springing from the volatility of thought, which forever escapes what it judges. Such license is resented by the zealous positivistic spirit and put down to mental disorder.

It was this misalliance, and the sneering empiricist sabotage loosed on me by those bearing the distasteful title of 'colleagues', that led to my being ejected from the Institute and landing in a low-rent bungalow in a small university town in the West, destitute of all influence and with scarcely enough resources to continue with my life-work. But my reduced situation is of no matter. He who offers for sale something unique that no-one wants to buy, represents, even against his will, freedom from exchange. Henceforth my existence can only be justified by upholding the constant responsibility of writing, which has become my last refuge against the brooding, festering horror to which morbid interests have laid me prone. The necessity to counter any slackening of intellectual tension with the utmost alertness, and to eliminate anything that has begun to encrust the work or to drift along idly – here is the only surety against creeping intoxication. There is no remedy but steadfast diagnosis of oneself; the attempt, through awareness, if not to escape this stark, morbid hatefulness that exceeds the foulest nightmares, at least to rob it of its dreadful violence, that of blindness.

Possibly I ought not to have studied so hard. Whether the dreams brought on the fever or the fever brought on the dreams, I do not know. What I can tell is that my sickness was instigated by that machine whose frantic, tinny cackle still echoes behind the walls of this dismal chamber with its brown hangings and maddening rows of antique tomes. Almost imperceptibly, as I drifted fitfully into sleep, the abstract horror of news and rumour spewed forth daily by the radiogram, and to which I had become passively accustomed, underwent a ghastly transmogrification into something altogether more distinct and unmistakably directed towards myself, but with a malignity whose eldritch proportions ruled out any merely personal malice. Indeed, I had the peculiar impression that the significance of the transmission owed to the very atomic structure of the radio phenomena itself, rather than to the message it conveyed. The latter consisted only in the administration of a peculiar kind of 'questionnaire', sinister in its banality and conducted in a hectoring and unspeakably abhorrent, quasi-ritualistic tone, like the collective drone of some loathsome gigantic insect hive ponderously shaped into the articulate speech of an alien species: *Has your wife a bodily ailment? Of what does your daily nourishment chiefly consist? Do you like jazz? Would it have been better to talk it over instead of beating up Curley? Who are the known associates of the subject 'Alright'? What are the principal causes of armchair cancer?* Then, dismal and shrill, like the piping of some amorphous idiot flute-player, there followed what any vaguely anthropoid being would hesitate to call 'music': Full of malignant cheer, as if an ingratiating commercial broadcast were serving as material for some elaborate psycho-technical experiment, its ghastly arias, constructed with deadly precision and deliberation, full of the mocking admonition to be happy, were swept aloft on great orchestrated swells obscenely distended with the gay promise of illusory gratification, their nauseating incantations violently devoid of all sense: *The cutlets are playing a dog's game, a dog's game; the cutlets are playing a dog's game, a dog's game; the cutlets are playing a dog's game, a dog's game, all the livelong day.*

I cannot say for how many nights these 'dream broadcasts' tormented me. No relief was to be had by severing the apparatus from its electrical source – for it was not thence that it drew its power – nor even by attempting, as I once did in a fit of rage against the relentless imbecility of this frightful din, to pulverize the machine itself by means of a powerful chainsaw.

As I tossed nightly in a state of agonized half-sleep, these emissions would mount to a climax of unbearable intensity. The inhuman prating became increasingly atomized, its turbid sequences subjected to a progressive statistical liquidation, and reaching their apex in a blasphemous domdaniel of cacophony, a satanic concert like six jazz plat-ters revolving at the same time. In that shrieking, the inmost soul of human fear and agony clawed hopelessly and insanely at the ebony gates of oblivion. Stark, utter horror burst over me and weighed my spirit with a black clutching panic from which it can never shake free. I awoke to red madness and the mockery of diabolism, as farther and farther down inconceivable vistas that phobic and crystalline anguish retreated and reverberated.

Upon sequestering myself in the library, for a time the loathsome titter of those infi-nitely appalling missives from beyond abated. Here I was able to continue my research, although the idea – somehow implanted by the demoniacal interrogations – of a black, hidden horror connected with incalculable gulfs of some sort of *distance*, was oddly persistent.

I began to have infrequent dreams of strange floatings over the city and through the re-gions around it. Certain brief, glimmering visions in these dreams – vague unplaceable dreams suggesting fragments of some hideous memory elaborately blotted out – now became connected irresistibly with the nature of the ominous 'transmissions'.

After a day marked by wild hope and deepest depression, I found myself in the open air, beneath an indescribable black sky full of scurrying clouds. It seemed to threaten imminent catastrophe. I glimpsed the entire panorama of the city stretched out before me, but compressed into a miniature space. It looked like a giant, prehistoric set of fortifications, with a few large industrial complexes (including two matching ones) in the middle. From afar I saw them protruding uncannily from the hillside as parts of a corpse may protrude from an ill-made grave. There were almost endless leagues of buildings, each in its garden, and ranged along paved roads fully two hundred feet wide. These units, developed regularly in fathomless vistas, were organized around the repetition of variously bizarrely-angled shapes. Once, I saw tremendous tessellated pools, reflecting the sun's rays onto the underside of colossal horizontal concrete canopies cantilevered immeasurable distances beyond their exterior columns. In the shrunken and gibbous sky three huge, menacing stars could be seen; they formed an isosceles triangle. Always, the whole scene was shot through with the same hopeless feeling of sorrow.

For some time I accepted the visions as natural, even though I had never before been an extravagant dreamer. In the course of some months, however, the element of terror figured with accumulating force when the dreams began so unfailingly to have the aspect of memories, and when my mind began to link them with my growing abstract disturbances – the feeling of mnemonic restraint, the curious impressions regarding time, the sense of a loathsome exchange with my secondary personality, and, considerably later, the inexplicable loathing of my own person.

In the depths of my worst depression since the winter months, I had these same dreams again, or, rather, I had dreams in which I remembered fragments of the first dreams. I have now again forgotten most of them, but I want to retain the pitiful vestiges I can remember in the hope that one day I shall perhaps remember more.

I was in a small room with a very high ceiling, a function room which was joined to the hall through connecting doors; a sort of foyer, with silvery tamarisks along the recessed walls at the rear and mesquite shade along the front walls. The folded structure covering this area resulted from the intersection of two gable roofs of problematical depth, their surface here and there vexed with anomalous spoutings. From a wide circle of ten scaffolds set up at regular intervals with a flame-girt monolith as a centre, eight concentric rings, monstrous constructions of black iridescent stone, each the hub of a system of five long, flat, triangularly-tapering arms, marked the passage from the tenebrous interior space to the noctilucous exterior. I was present at a large, unusually lavish banquet. The rooms and tables were lit only by candles that burned with a disturbingly livid incandescence, and this made it difficult to find one's way to the main table. I struck out in search of my place on my own, pacing through Cyclopean corridors, black labyrinths so complex that no retracing of my steps could even be considered, up and down gigantic inclined planes of the same monstrous masonry leading to roof gardens covered with arcades of structural members, and through chambers clad in white marble and gold-plated tiles and replete with curious and inexplicable utensils of myriad sorts. Then there were colossal caverns of intricate machinery whose outlines and purpose were wholly strange to me, and vast shelves of some lustrous metal, bearing odious oblong boxes of disturbing size. The whole of this deranged complex indicated unmistakeably a level of scientific knowledge far exceeding that of our race, but of a wholly alien cast, and entirely evacuated of the familiar furnishings of civilisation. In these malevolent palaces were no casement windows to open, but only sliding frames to shove, no gentle latches but turnable handles, no forecourt, no doorstep before the street, no wall around the garden.

Eventually I found myself on a high, fantastically balustraded terrace about a boundless jungle of outlandish, incredible peaks, like the battlemented lookout platform of a tower above which the spire rises up still higher. It was with a grim sense of foreboding that I began to clamber up the spire. It was very steep, difficult and dangerous, something halfway between a spiral staircase and an Alpine chimney, the air inside thick with the stifling odor of nether gulfs. After an infinity of awesome, sightless crawling, I found that there was scarcely any room for me inside the spire. I was now gripped by panic.

From this perspective, on the plain below I saw groups of people with apparatuses, some kind of surveyors perhaps, functionaries whose entire mien was heavy with the pall of some unspeakable disaster. Grey, twisted and brittle, a mixture of riff-raff and monstrosities, dwarflike figures with bald heads and tentacles that awakened veiled suggestions of a monstrous plasticity – their countless hordes were, as it seemed, doomed to labour endlessly beneath the vaulted heights of those Olympian edifices in a kind of post-existence, like cancerous appendages dragged along by the monotonous, obtuse voracity of their blind mechanical striving.

Even in occasional sites where these dismal beings gathered to indulge in some odious festive rite, their manipulated intoxication, their torchlight processions, their drumbeating, were arid and joyless as the eldritch scurrying of fiend-born rats across carrion-black pits of sawed, picked bones and opened skulls. Yet in the petrified otherness of these non-entities, there was something unmistakeably venal: as neutralized and impotent as ignominious ballast whilst engaged in their futile ministrations, during these impious pageants their eyes took on a manic yet cold look of grasping, devouring, commandeering. And their measured gait, the hideous equivalence of their impeccably-calibrated actions, the implacable way in which they carried out their silent errands, were belied by an foreboding sense of the ancient, dread rituals whose gestures their fixed and empty motions seemed unknowingly to mime.

As the strange cadences of their leering imprecations were carried up to me on the black wind gusting foully from that distant plain, I realized with a jolt of grotesque disbelief that these same impotent labourers had been the conductors of my nocturnal dream-broadcasts. At the same moment I became aware, with a sense of horror and oppression which threatened to master, paralyze and annihilate me, that the antediluvian source of their ossified habitudes, a starkly horrific thing incommensurable with the horizons of any individual experience and having long since disappeared, for them, into the merciful abyss of forgetfulness, was yet present. There, sprawling repulsively across the plain, tended by the countless viscous masses of self-oblivious drones, I saw It. I cannot even hint what it was like, for it was a compound of all that is repellent, uncanny, unwelcome, abnormal, and detestable. A mostly liquescent horror, thick with the ghoulish shade of decay, antiquity, and dissolution; the putrid, dripping eidolon of unwholesome revelation, the awful baring of that which the merciful earth should always hide; something blind and mutilated, endlessly calling to itself with a terrible moan that reverberated throughout untold chasms of unknown space, a renunciatory cry which, in that abysmally unexpected moment, I knew as also being my own – the ventriloquizing tongue of a vile heredity slavering venomously at me from beyond all humanly-thinkable time. An unspeakable melancholy, drawing me irresistibly into the abyss, awakened this old, impotently yearning sound in its depths.

In my panic, I tried feebly to croak a desperate warning to the sacrificial hordes below, as if my words could somehow undo their enigmatic readiness to fall under the sway of the unnamable Thing's absolute domination. But my speech seemed awkward and foreign. I used my vocal organs clumsily and gropingly, and my diction had a curiously stilted quality, as if I had laboriously learned the English language from books. The pronunciation was barbarously alien, whilst the idiom seemed to include both scraps of curious archaism and expressions of a wholly incomprehensible cast. Language sent back to me like an echo the humiliation which my immeasurable dread had inflicted on me in forgetting what I was.

The scene melted away, and I was swept by a black wind through gulfs of fathomless grey with the needle-like pinnacles of unknown mountains miles below me. After a while there was utter blackness, and then the light of myriad stars forming strange, alien constellations.

These events seemed so vivid to me that I found it hard to decide whether I had really experienced them. That is precisely the pattern that operates when one is gripped by madness. The creeping malignity of that vast abomination pursues me still, and I cannot shake off the conviction that, in contemplating these appalling parched vistas of the unbroken reign of glacial death, I had become irretrievably aware of something forgotten: The lingering awareness of an ancient wound, belonging to some other plane or phase of entity from which it once fell, vintigillions of aeons ago.

With this certainty, the sway of reason is irrefutably shaken. Nothing will protect me from the black sickness. The centre of intellectual self-discipline as such is in the process of decomposition. I know where I am but I cannot feel myself in the place where I find myself. Faced by a terrible cataract of memory – the awakening of thought to the nightmare of those unplumbed strata of extra-cosmic history – faced with the memory of a forgetting that had better have been left in place, the commemoration of that Thing whose internment in the deepest recesses of desuetude was once the very guarantee of my sanity, has become my only imperative.

A consciousness that wishes to withstand the unspeakable finds itself again and again thrown back on the attempt to understand, if it is not to succumb subjectively to the madness that prevails objectively. He who relinquishes awareness of the growth of horror not merely succumbs to cold-hearted contemplation, but fails to perceive, together with the specific difference between the newest and that preceding it, the true identity of the whole, of terror without end. Paralyzed by fear of the truth, mankind deigns not to raise the stone under which the monster lies brooding; to release to stark consciousness the whole process they have undertaken to suppress – yet unconsciously advance. In willing not to know that we serve Them still, that They shall awake and once again claim Their own, we condemn the spirit to increasing darkness. The world is systematized horror, its essence is abomination. Loathsomeness waits and dreams in the deep, and decay spreads over the tottering cities of men. To repress, in the face of this state of affairs, the full awareness of what has happened and what is behind it, may itself contribute to the recurrence of the unspeakable at any place on earth.

Still I dream. Once again, I am falling from those Cyclopean towers through deep, foetid shafts of reticulated ebony-black space, rushing past constellations whose form I cannot make out. Crashing down, I am pursued by the mocking laughter of the insidious object that disempowered me, liquidating intellect and pulverizing individuality.

Some day a new constellation will form, and as this constellation sheds its deathly-livid light on the most distant past, we may finally decipher the black knowledge that festers in the chasms of chthonic subconsciousness, molded by the dead brain of a hybrid nightmare – the diabolical unknown.

REASON WITHOUT REASON

Amanda Beech & Jaspar Joseph-Lester

JJ-L: I think this might be a good moment to turn more directly to the work you have made for *Sanity Assassin*. You speak of the world authored by us, but in your work these subjectivities are aimed at particular narratives derived from Critical Theory, the narratives that extend from it, references to the violence of U.S. pulp-fiction-style anti-heroes and cinematic representations of subjectivity. We have talked at some length about Shulman and how his images of LA are embedded in a wider ideological framework that seeks to impose an anti-humanist ontology. Perhaps you could now say more about how this is brought into conflict with the other spatial, theoretical and political subjectivities and narratives that are played out in the exhibition? Or perhaps more specifically, could you say more about how you stage what we might now describe as an uneasy coexistence of representational systems?

AB: The interests that were driving this work were particularly rooted in understanding the production of certain narrative spaces, but most particular to this was how images and theories produce what we understand LA to be now, in its social, aesthetic and political configuration. I wanted to think about how attempts to produce dissonance, critical distance and resistance to LA culture per se, mirror its cult of individualism, and produce a concept of nature that actually informs the traits of a neo-liberal self-organising politics. This production of LA culture takes place not only through its material architectural space but, of course, through the ideological positions and territories that produce that space and are demarcated by it. In the work I wanted to consider what can be crudely described as two ways of approaching LA as 'given reality':

two forms of realism that are both, in the end, false. These are proposed in the work through reflecting on and extending the work of Adorno and Horkheimer's dialectical theory, which tried to rationalise and rescue the subject from self-annihilation, from a destruction at the hands of our own nature, our predilection to reason. This narrative was then opened up to the acceptance of this as the *only nature*; a connectedness that de-centres subjectivity on the one hand and recuperates it on the other. I think this move is retraced in our conversation about Shulman's work and his mastery of nature. In the latter an encounter with reality is written as physical violence, and in the former it is suicidal private horror. One of the reasons for titling the work *Sanity Assassin* is that the work examines how the consequences of both these rationalisations of reality wreck a concept of sanity. This led me to ask how we can think through reason without reason as its principle or article of faith, whilst understanding that this does not derail reason itself.

With this in mind, during the development of the work I began to get more concerned with how nature played a central role in theories that have looked to 'reason out' the human condition in relation to it. This not only involved Adorno and Horkheimer's *Dialectic of Enlightenment* (1947), but also Adorno's *Dream Notes* (2007), a diary of his dreams written during his time in LA. The fear of culture as a process of mimesis that produced a dialectic of reason and barbarism was apparent in both sets of writing – it was present in his dreams that were 'as black as death' as much as in his academic work. In the latter, the dialectic is expressed in the final synthesis: the (often erotic) horror of becoming culture-nature, where subjectivities are made indistinct from their milieu. And his dreams are tantalised by the violence of this possibility, and flirt with the correspondences between the most banal everyday objects and the ultimate classifications of horror. There is no need to interpret these dreams into the world of Adorno's philosophy, because for me they are simply part of the same psychology. Extending from these dreams and within the *Dialectic of Enlightenment*, Adorno and Horkheimer's reclamation of reason seeks to overcome the problem of mimesis, but this process paradoxically signals *another reason* and with that *another nature* that goes unaccounted for in the work. This nature without culture, and reason disassociated from nature, prefigures a network of correspondences, schematics and causal relations that require a ruthless organisation, and which produce their own drama. This becomes a web of managed distances that I wanted to think through in the work, as well as this process of absolute synthesis that is written as the true horror for Adorno's politics. These notions of distance are spoken of very differently when we reflect back on Shulman's realism, but nevertheless what stands out for me is how these ideas, images and comprehensions of the condition of human agency seem to articulate similar forms of spatial organisation – space thought in terms of privacy and seclusion, security and territorialisation. An issue that was there at the start of the project and remains an issue for me, then, is how to deal with the actual forms of securitisation that are produced by these varying critiques, and which seem to standardise how we understand, identify and recognise power right now.

For example, if we look at Frank Gehry's *Goldwyn Branch Library* (1983-6) in Hollywood, which adopts the architecture of a fortress-style build, we can see a clear irony at work in that the building reminds us of the social and aesthetic configurations of public space, especially in the LA context. However, what is problematic about this irony is that it seems to reproduce the same forms of power that it cites as the object of its critique. Mike Davis also wrote about this in his book *City of Quartz* (1992), but unlike Davis what I am interested in here is how producing this politics has a connection to a certain form of humanism that needs to be critiqued. I don't think Davis moves past this in his work. Therefore, one of the questions I still have is how images, objects, buildings and art have affect in reconfiguring and constructing identities that do not underscore the normative forms and conditions that we have just discussed.

Frank Gehry, *Goldwyn Branch Library*, 1983-6, Hollywood, California, USA

JJ-L: The fortress function of LA architecture is striking, not least in John Portman's *Bonaventure Hotel* (1976). Davis' critique of what Fredric Jameson has termed a 'fully blown postmodern building' tells us much about the problem with humanism and how, as you point out, it fails to take responsibility for determining the very object of its critique. This contradiction - critique being both a means to contest and construct systems of power – can be argued to possess some agency when we begin to understand critique as a force that is fluid and unfixed (and not, as with Davis, tied to an unchanging monolithic ideological framework). How does this notion of agency inform the type of experiences that you set out to produce in your work?

AB: The question of what critique is, and can be, has been central to my work for a long time. It is often the subject matter of the work, but it is also something that is speculatively proposed by the work, in that I'm interested in what formulations and operations critique can take on without any investment in causality or instrumentality or any such grieving process that might articulate the disappearance of 'meaning'. I think the irony that Davis critiques in Gehry, and along with it, as you point out, Davis's humanism, both play on theories of proximity and distance. They both establish an identification with, or a resistance to, the object of their critique. This topography of critique underscores the power it seeks to undermine and even produces the domination that it had hoped to unsettle. In this sense, exposing power and making it visible simply reminds us that power exists as such. It is often claimed, by the political right and left, that without such an object of resistance, either there will be unbridled anarchy or, on the other hand, actually existing power structures will escape unquestioned. But these shared anxieties are the result of simple formalisms that do not, I think, understand power as contingent. With this in mind, the work explores the various contradictions that are produced as a consequence of theorising how to act when there is no absolute power to target and no centre from which to operate. Most particularly, the work attempted to explore the aestheticisation and theorisation of this infinitude as the real of the political and how it informs and shapes politics. The aesthetic that this produces in the history of politics and aesthetics is double: a psychological horror of this reality, and a physical violence that embodies it.

The work takes us into this double narrative with due garish intensity, bringing the two aesthetics into a competing sphere that allows me to form *another whole*. Whilst these competing voices are fragments, they are equally motivated to make their power exacting, and they share a particular faith in the subject's ability to rationalise its place within its milieu; a milieu that is an incredible compression of the ontic and the ontological, because the local and temporal actions of each subject are hinged upon a universal understanding of a (human) nature. The organisation of the work as an installation is key to this question, as it is here that we encounter the work as three screens that are always filled with information. Each screen takes on different parts of the narrative and leaves them as autonomous voices that share the same space. The voices do not mingle absolutely, since they are not forced together; but neither do they operate in some form of antagonism. Instead they are seen serially, as if they replace each other or overwrite each other. The architecture of the screens is central to this configuration: each is seen as a discrete object set within the gallery at different angles and heights. Each set of image sequences comes together in a monumental redux of a cityscape/cinematic experience that references the industry of image production and mass consumption. The installation as a whole also shifts in reference from interior to exterior, as for the first exhibition of this work at Spike Island, Bristol, in January 2010, the work takes on the form of a larger installation. The first part sees a series of vintage metal chainsaws displayed on a large white plinth with a mirrored top, and was inspired by the McCulloch chainsaw company's foyer in LA, a public and yet private space. It was also the subject of a set of Shulman prints. The space for the video work is choreographed much more in terms of the dynamics of public space, where the architectural framework of the screens and their supports establish a space where the viewer can move around, change angles, and see the work from different spatial perspectives. In fact the video instructs this as part of its operation. The viewer must be able to shift focus like this because the work demands that this happen as action shifts in focus from one screen to another. The mobile subject is subjected by the work precisely because of this appeal to the choice of vantage points.

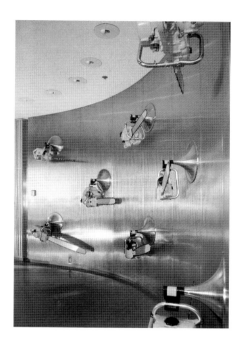

Julius Shulman, *McCulloch Motors, Office & Showroom, LA*, 1957

I think this connection between the subject matter of the work and how that is materialised as an artwork helps me to answer your question. Critique, as I propose it here, is the operation of both representation and demonstration, or image and action and primarily in my work I understand critique as an operation of rhetorical force. It seems here we might come back to the force of will, but this is not the same as the mysticism that we see in Shulman or Adorno. Instead, within the work, both Shulman and Adorno are taken as starting points that are then garbled, extended, blown up and collapsed with other fictions inspired by other LA narratives. One of the things that the work looked to was the TV series *Columbo*. Peter Falk plays the dishevelled New York homicide cop antagonising with inimitable passivity the lives of guilty, rich, upper bourgeois and blue blood Angelenos. The arrogance of power is expressed not only in murder, but in the decadent locations, the modernist interiors of dark wood and silver metal, screens, rugs, glass, sweeping drives, swimming pools, lush foliage, servants, hard drinks in thick glasses, easy chairs, towels and cigarettes. Also furnishing the scene, just as in Shulman's work, we see chrysanthemums used as props – the yellow kind that you see at funerals. These pull the world of the TV cop show together with the choreography of Shulman's America – a world of seamless dream power. The work extended this to work through these conceptions of singularity, with the jive talk of LA noir: those narratives that figure for us the heroes of liberal democracy.

James Ellroy characterises this with jarring conviction in the preface of his book *Blood's A Rover* (2009), the last in his LA trilogy that takes America as its subject. In this book, as elsewhere, Ellroy presents the force of his own authorship as equal to the work of the characters he depicts. This self-representation does not relegate the text, or his voice, to the level of unreal fiction. Nor does it retreat to an appeal to the individual nature of subjectivity (which after all is always a false apology that believes that truth claims are non-constraining: *it is only 'I' who claim this and you are free to agree or not*). Instead it is intolerant and forceful, because it claims truth, destroying that old necessity to distinguish between fact and fiction as the beating heart of a knowledge we must possess. Ellroy's work points to how art's critique must articulate the persistence of the transcendent subject that authors worlds in the context of contingency: something that *Sanity Assassin* lives out in the same dimensions of fiction, truth, rhetoric and violence. As a politics of contingency unhooks us from the correspondence between foundations, schematics and value systems and the Real, it also presses us now more urgently towards new facts.

AMERICA:
I window-peeped for years of our History. It was one long mobile stakeout and kick-the-door-in shakedown. I had a license to steal and a ticket to ride. I followed people. I bugged and tapped and caught big events in ellipses. I remained unknown. My surveillance links the Then to the Now in a never-before-revealed manner. I was there. My reportage is buttressed by credible hearsay and insider tattle. Massive paper trails provide verification. This book derives from stolen public files and usurped private journals. It is the sum of personal adventure and forty years of scholarship. I am a literary executor and an agent provocateur. I did what I did and saw what I saw and learned my way through to the rest of the story.
You carry the seed of belief within you already. You recall the time this narrative captures and sense conspiracy. I am here to tell you that it is all true and not at all what you think.
You will read with some reluctance and capitulate in the end. The following pages will force you to succumb.
I am going to tell you everything.

JJ-L: The relation between image, action and the space of rhetorical force is bound to a notion of persuasiveness. This was evident throughout the campaign for the American presidency, where arguments were won and lost on the basis of their rhetorical affect. The influence of American culture and, in particular, the formation of power viewed through American culture, is evident throughout your work. We have discussed how this staging of culture returns us to broader notions of the political but perhaps you could say a bit more about how you think these representations of post-war American culture are bound to an expanded notion of materiality.

AB: The force of language in US politics is exemplified in election campaigns where the presidential debates are televised live and are gauged in an up-to-the-minute set of correspondences between the performance of particular political arguments and the changes and fluctuations of the voting curve of the population. This is a measure that *only counts*, whilst at the same time it rationalises and organises language into numbers, and then into power. The correspondence that the measure claims in itself contains no guarantees that any particular language can win assent more than any other. Here we can see the double aspect of language as rhetorical force: language seeks to persuade or to move others to agreement, but at the same time there is no systematic connection between its cause and its effect. Meaning is therefore an entanglement of the representational, mobile and temporal, making language commensurate with force and force with language. So, yes, this is an expanded notion of materiality since we are not speaking in terms of a phenomenology of objects, but instead of an encounter with the force of particular languages and ideas and their conviction. As we come up against other languages, other systems of belief, we acknowledge their force as law. We exercise our own beliefs with the same conviction.

But what we also see in the presidential debates (and here I am thinking of the live debates between Obama and McCain that I watched in LA whilst I was filming the work) is a particular manoeuvring around already-identifiable principles that are central to liberal notions of governmentality. The liberal principle of freedom is the self-constraint of the democratic debate producing the place where meaning is gauged. I think America, and particularly LA, exemplifies the problem of political principles more sharply and becomes a useful case study for politics, mostly because of the marginal imaginations of what the political can be. This is what I encountered when talking about these issues with the people I met whilst in LA, whose politics was still defined by the fear of becoming *too Continental* (and they didn't have philosophy in mind!). This protectionism in many ways reminds me of Thomas Hobbes's *Leviathan* (1651). However, where in Hobbes the State secures political liberty with material and symbolic power, in neo-liberal democracy the State is disintegrated to the point of the sham symbolic, but it is still called upon as the place that can manufacture the political necessities of freedom and security. The distribution of power through language is also relevant to Hobbes and his theory of rhetorical power, where although for Hobbes language has force, some languages have more force than others. To win assent in speechmaking, one must invoke the polemics of heaven and hell, and/or good and evil. This will wow the audience. Following this excitement and fear, the speechmaker must offer a measured personal voice as the objective reasoned voice of mediocrity. To win power one must achieve this balance of drama, morality and sense-making. A little more recently, performative speech theories, such as those in the work of Judith Butler and Jacques Derrida, demonstrate an abiding attention to a schematics of meaning in another form that privileges the direct speech-act over more mediated forms of presentation. Paradoxically, the attempt to find a language that is capable of unlocking the potential of language itself, by either cutting through or manipulating language systems produces correspondences between reality and referent similar to those it had hoped to override or command. The prevalence of a structural schematics of language, that an expanded notion of materiality breaks with, points to the political problem when it comes to language. That is, how can we actually access this expanded notion of materiality and its promise of other potentialities when the in-expansive order and reason of our liberty seems to constrain us more than ever?

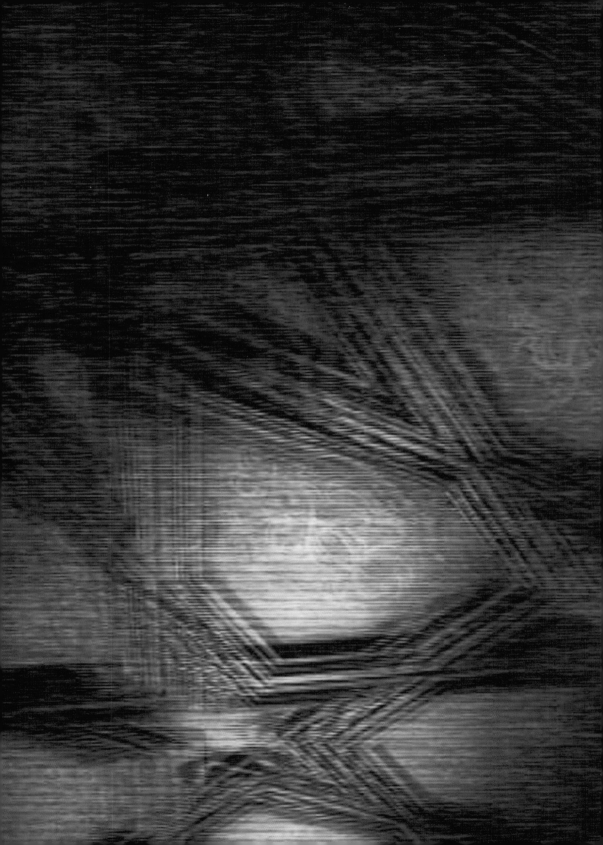

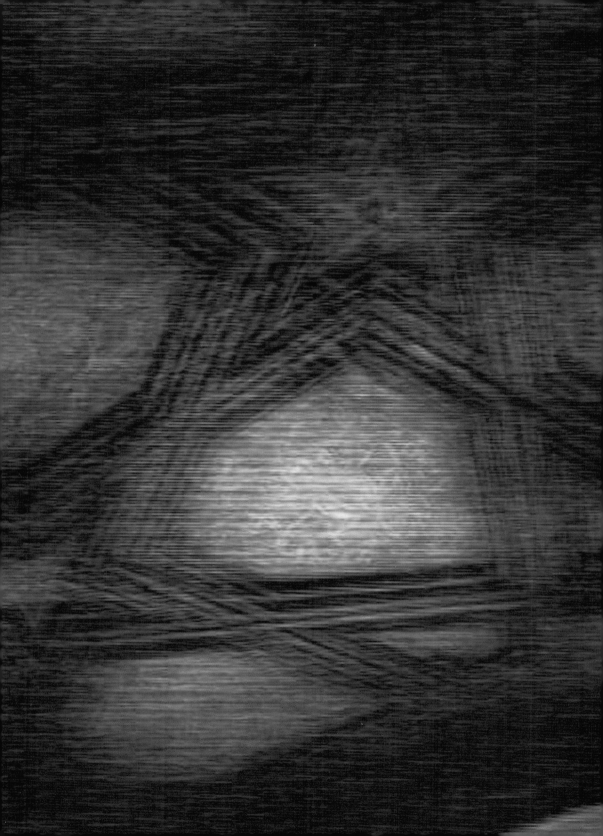

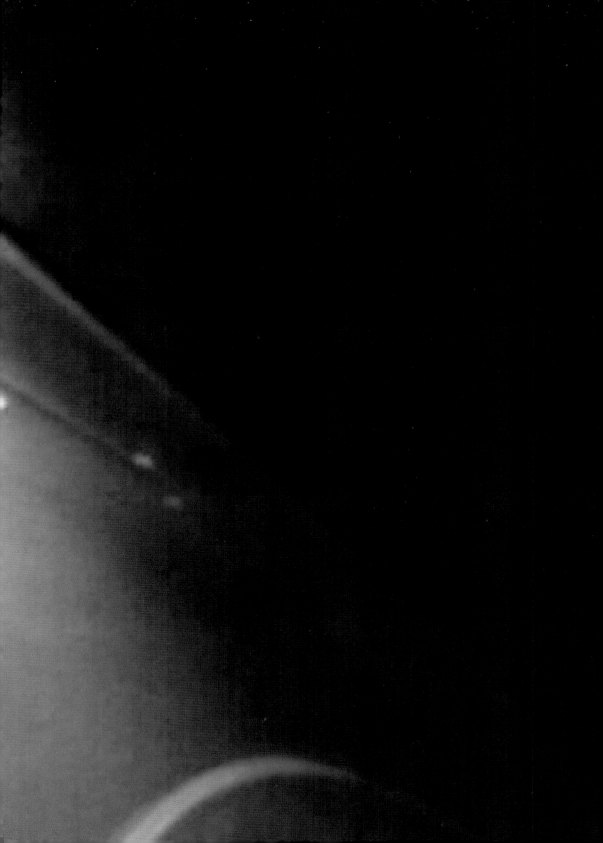